The
THORN
NECKLACE

Self-Portrait with Thorn Necklace and Hummingbird,
1940 by Frida Kahlo. Credit: Erich Lessing / Art Resource, NY.

The
THORN
NECKLACE

Healing Through Writing *and* the Creative Process

Francesca Lia Block

SEAL PRESS

Seal Press
1700 Fourth Street
Berkeley, California
www.sealpress.com

Printed in the United States of America
First edition: May 2018

Published by Seal Press, an imprint of Perseus Books, LLC, a subsidiary of Hachette Book Group, Inc. The Seal Press name and logo is a trademark of the Hachette Book Group.

The Hachette Speakers Bureau provides a wide range of authors for speaking events. To find out more, go to www.hachettespeakersbureau.com or call (866) 376-6591.

The publisher is not responsible for websites (or their content) that are not owned by the publisher.

Interior Design: Linda Mark

Library of Congress Cataloging-in-Publication Data
Names: Block, Francesca Lia author.
Title: The thorn necklace : healing through writing and the creative process / Francesca Lia Block ; foreword by Grant Faulkner.
Description: Berkeley : Seal Press, 2018. |
Identifiers: LCCN 2017043732 (print) | LCCN 2017048230 (ebook) | ISBN 9781580057523 (ebook) | ISBN 9781580057516 (hardback)
Subjects: LCSH: Creative writing. | Authorship--Technique. | Creation (Literary, artistic, etc.) | Block, Francesca Lia. | BISAC: BIOGRAPHY & AUTOBIOGRAPHY / Personal Memoirs. | REFERENCE / Writing Skills. | SELF-HELP / Creativity. | SELF-HELP / Personal Growth / Self-Esteem.
Classification: LCC PN189 (ebook) | LCC PN189 .B65 2018 (print) | DDC 808.02--dc23
LC record available at https://lccn.loc.gov/2017043732

ISBNs: 978-1-5800-5751-6 (hardcover), 978-1-5800-5752-3 (ebook)

LSC-C

10 9 8 7 6 5 4 3 2 1

For my family
and for Dr. Carol Blake

CONTENTS

FOREWORD

—— Four Simple Words

Grant Faulkner

"I AM A WRITER."

They're just four simple words. Yet many of us have difficulty saying them, no matter where we are on our creative journeys.

I know I did. In my early days as a writer, when people asked me what I did, I hesitated to tell them because I knew I'd have to endure an inevitable cross-examination. People asked me how many books I'd published. They asked me how I planned to make a living writing. Or they just said, "Oh," and kept their thoughts to themselves. Few applauded the fact that I was devoting my life to my creativity.

Every writer has experienced such moments.

When these inevitable moments came for me, I would try to dodge my way out. I squirmed. I mumbled. I fled.

Writing was my religion, my foremost purpose in life, my consolation. But as the years passed and I didn't have the successes that others deemed the qualifications of a "real" writer, I went into hiding. I wrote, but I lost the strength of my words. I wrote, but with a doubt that needled each sentence, a lack of self-confidence that clouded my imagination. My boldness evaporated. My verve started to become a distant memory. I lost my truth.

The path to holding onto your truth is charted in this book. If I had read *The Thorn Necklace* then, maybe I would have struggled less. I know I would have written more, and the more I write, the more satisfying my life becomes.

But somewhere within me, without even knowing it, I must have believed that "other people" were "real" writers. I understand this syndrome well now. As executive director of National Novel Writing Month, I talk to thousands of people each year about their creative lives, and I hear too many people diminish themselves as writers. They aren't *really* writers, they say, because they aren't pedigreed with MFAs, or they haven't published a book, or they don't go to cocktail parties with other writers in Brooklyn. They tell me they're not creative types, or that they don't have time to write in a busy life, or that they've been ridiculed for having the audacity to think they could write a novel.

But when you tell yourself such things, a gate falls down between your self and your creativity, and once that gate falls down, it can be a heavy thing to lift. It can be so heavy that you might give up.

If you *don't* give up, if you keep that gate lifted high, your life becomes enriched in otherwise unimaginable ways. This is the beautiful lesson of Francesca Lia Block's captivating study of the writing life, the book you are holding in your hands.

When we turn away from our creative souls, Francesca presages, we unwittingly harm ourselves. When we don't lay claim to our creative impulse to share what we believe to be true about ourselves and the world around us, an agony festers from self-diminishment, and another thorn is added to the daily existence that encircles us.

You tell yourself that your story isn't interesting enough to be written on paper. You tell yourself that other people will laugh at you. You tell yourself that you should be an adult and fix that squeaky front door or paint your living room or at least wash the dishes. You should be practical, filling your life with all kinds of "shoulds."

Writing a story can feel like a trivial entertainment, a whimsical activity that shouldn't have a significant place in a busy adult's life. But that's forgetting one thing. When you minimize your expression, you minimize who you are. When you tell yourself that your story isn't important, you make it so.

The Thorn Necklace reminds me that we are born to be creators, so we need to approach each day with a creative mindset. When I had children, I loved watching the kids play at preschool. They created out of impulse, without thought, without any notion of whether the final product would be good or bad. Put a canvas in front of them and lay out some finger paints, and they would plunge in with gusto, not worrying about any mess because they reveled in the wonders of the colors. They painted with unfettered glee, unconcerned by anyone's opinion because they were so immersed in the story they were telling.

As I watched them, it was hard to think that they might not be equally as zealous and wildly creative as adults. I worried that they would experience a creative scar. Perhaps someone would tell them they weren't artistic. Perhaps the more practical matters of life would tamp down their imaginative spark.

I've learned that you might stuff your story down to the bottom of your to-do list or try to abandon it on the side of a highway, but your story won't go away. Your story needs to be told. As Francesca assures us, if you listen, it's always whispering within you, if not crying for attention. It wants to be brought to life. It wants to breathe. It wants you to put your hands in the paints of your words and color the canvas.

We are storytellers because stories are the vehicles we navigate the world with. Writing a story is many things: a quest, a prayer, a hunger, a tantrum, a revolt, an escape that ironically leads you back to yourself. We need our stories because our stories connect us to other people. We need our stories because our stories connect us to ourselves. When you claim your creativity, when you say, "I am a writer," it becomes a vital part of your identity. You're not only braver on the page, you're also braver in the rest of your life because you're a change agent, a builder of new worlds.

As I read *The Thorn Necklace*, I thought about all of this. I thought about how every writer needs to constantly remind themselves of the value of their creativity not because of books published or awards received, but simply because they show up to conjure stories and string words together on the page. Block beautifully explores the urgent value of one's creativity and how our stories can be transformative life-giving forces. If we don't write our stories, how will we truly know who we are? How will we define the world? How will we touch the mysteries of life?

"There is no greater agony than bearing an untold story inside you," said Maya Angelou.

You don't want to die with the anguish of an untold story in your heart. It's time to say you're a writer—and to write your story. With *The Thorn Necklace*, you'll see how with every word you write on the page, you're cultivating meaning. That's important because our stories—Francesca's, yours, and mine—are the candles that light up the darkness that life can become.

INTRODUCTION
—— You Are an Artist!

MY FATHER HAD ALWAYS SUPPORTED MY CREATIVE EN-
deavors, but I never knew how much until, weak with
radiation treatments, his frail voice boomed through the ear-
piece of the dorm room telephone. "You are a writer!"

I stood clinging to the phone like a lifeline. Black-
mascara tears streaked my face and my stomach hurt from
the mounds of white rice and tofu I ate each night in the
cafeteria and the copious amounts of liquor the dorm RAs
had provided to their underage charges the night before.
More tears poured from my eyes and trickled saltily into my
mouth, but they were different this time. Gratitude. Relief.
Possibility. In that moment, my father had given me what I
wanted and needed more than almost anything else in the
world.

A month earlier, my parents had driven me up to UC Berkeley. Dusty oleander bushes lined the I-5; we passed a cattle ranch that reeked with the stench of fear and death. But late summer sunshine lit the streets of Berkeley, melting through the leaves of box elders and copper beech trees over the campus and surrounding buildings. My room was on the eighth floor of the dorm. Months later someone would offer me LSD in that room and I would turn it down; considering my fragile state of mind, I knew the combination might be lethal. On the day of my arrival, I already felt a great sense of despair.

My mother helped me put posters on the wall above the narrow bed—Monet's water lilies, David Bowie as Aladdin Sane, Frida Kahlo in her thorn necklace, The Sex Pistols, Marilyn Monroe, James Dean and his lookalike, Picasso's Blue Period Saltimbanque. They both squinted and pouted and showed off their cheekbones but the latter wore a wreath of roses and held a pipe with an effetely sensual turn of the wrist. All these images were intended as talismans against loneliness and the homesickness I'd suffered since childhood, even when I left my family for a single night.

We ate dinner at the Good Earth—sweet, fragrant tea with our "seventies health food" meal of brown rice, cashew chicken stir fry, and a salad with alfalfa sprouts. Since my father's illness my mother had become increasingly health conscious, serving us whole grains and organic fruits and vegetables and cutting back on red meat and rich cheeses. I thought of this as the last meal, an end to the comforts of my mother's cooking and my parents' home. The food left a bitter taste in my mouth that lingered as I said goodbye.

I looked forward to the solace of a poetry class but my professor was not easily impressed. As we sat in the classroom in Wheeler Hall, a stately building with Doric columns lining its façade and echoing, arched hallways within, he talked about the poetry of Pound, Eliot, Yeats, and H.D., and taught us the importance of using a symbolic image to express emotion rather than trying to describe the emotion itself. My teacher sang the praises of my lyrical, spectacled and freckled neighbor in her mod mini and pointed patent leather flats, but when my turn came he looked at me sternly.

"There's nothing like a noun," he told me. "Get rid of all those adjectives. They show you don't trust your reader."

His words weren't that harsh but my skin was thin (literally; I've always been prone to sunburns, freckles, moles, and acne) and my homesick nerves were flayed with fear about losing my father.

My professor was right about the adjectives and nouns. It was one of the best things I learned from him (even though I often still break the rule). But what my father told me afterward mattered more.

You are a writer.

I believe what he said in that moment, and my parents' encouragement of my creativity since my birth, made it possible for me to become a successful artist.

> I've written to transform pain, to save my mind from its incessant loopings, to save my life.

At twenty-seven I published my first book and have continued to put out about a book a year (young adult, adult fiction, short stories, poetry, memoir, erotica) for three decades. I was able to quit my jobs in a clothing store and an art gallery and support myself exclusively through my art for many years. I've been translated into Japanese, German, Italian, French, Norwegian, Swedish, Finnish, Portuguese, Bulgarian, and Turkish, and I've won a number of awards, including a lifetime achievement award from the American Library Association for my magical realist LA family saga.

My limited stint as a journalist allowed me to hang out with Tori Amos for a weekend in the English countryside, interview Perry Farrell, and have an intimate chat with Joseph Gordon-Levitt on a nearly deserted UCLA campus (he even offered me his jacket against the cold). The screenplay I wrote based on my first book got me meetings with David Lynch at his home in the Hollywood Hills and Juno Temple at a Silver Lake café (I brought her a bouquet of pink lilies as tall as she is), interest from Tim Burton's company and actor/writer/director John Cameron Mitchell (*Hedwig and the Angry Inch*), and an option from Fox Searchlight and Steven Spielberg, who walked up at an Amblin party and told me my book, about a bleach blond punk pixie flowerchild looking for love in 1980s Los Angeles with her gay best friend, was like a contemporary *Rebel Without a Cause*.

Glamorous young screenwriters and directors and Pulitzer prize–winning authors have worked on film adaptations of my books. A theater company in Chicago produced two plays from my work. I participated in an all-night shoot of a short based on my "Bluebeard" retelling at a pink mansion in the Oakland hills.

Women and men have tattooed my words on their bodies; named themselves, their pets, and their bands after my characters; met their best friends through my books; and devoted websites and blogs to my writing. One couple told me they read a passage from one of my books to each other at their wedding. Their sunflower-faced young children had accompanied them to my bookstore appearance, and their precocious nine-year-old daughter read the wedding passage aloud for the audience.

"You're our muse," the couple said. "We met online looking for someone to go to punk shows with and both listed your books as an influence."

In spite of my own personal struggles with sustaining love relationships, fans have told me that my stories helped shape their romantic ideals and set them on successful quests to find their own "Secret Agent Lovers." Pierced-nosed waitresses at restaurants recognize my name on the credit card and tell me they moved to LA because of how I wrote about it in my books.

When I reach out to my devoted, loyal online community of fans and friends, I receive immediate responses from around the world. Models, fashion designers, photographers, graphic artists, actors, filmmakers, musicians, and other writers have offered me their services, thanking me for inspiring them.

They come to my home with their pink hair and rhinestones and platform shoes, their angel wings and purses full of puppies. They help me with odd jobs and bring me gifts—perfumes, chapbooks, zines, crystals, flowers, music mixes, and homemade jewelry with mystical properties. Tarot readings and love spells are performed.

A restaurant in Seattle created an entire menu based on my stories. I've even gotten to experience my childhood dream of working in fashion when my name briefly appeared on the labels of Wildfox, a well-known clothing line, and I also helped design, produce, and market a small line of my own.

MY LIFE AS a writer has been a grimoire, a kind of magic book. And all this is greatly due to my parents' encouragement.

Of course, I was very fortunate; not everyone has this kind of support. Even parents, mentors, or friends with the most loving intentions have their reasons to dissuade a budding creative from his or her dream.

Will she make enough money? Will he be disappointed? Heartbroken? Less conscious reasons to discourage a loved one might include a parent or teacher's own history of frustration and fear.

My Secret Man was praised by a teacher for his writing skills around the same time in his childhood as a teacher noticed mine, but when he went home and told his father that he wanted to be a writer, he was met with: "Prepare to go hungry." He's been valiantly fighting these words ever since.

FOR THE LAST ten years, I've been focusing on giving others what my father gave me. Not only am I interested in teaching about **plot**, **character**, **setting**, **style**, and **voice** in a supportive but challenging way, but more importantly I want to be the mentor who shouts, "You are

> Life might be hard, but art? This we can do. Together.

a writer! Write! Read! Work hard! Don't despair! Never give up! You have something of value to share with the world!"

With desire, hard work, and commitment I believe you can be successful at expressing yourself and telling your story. All you need is a little support.

As humans, maybe that's all any of us need.

Personally, I've survived anorexia, anxiety, depression, two miscarriages, divorce, the near loss of my home, the death of both parents from cancer, and the loss of half the vision in one eye, all with the help of my writing and the community it has given me.

In her book *The Midnight Disease*, Alice Flaherty coins the term "hypergraphia" and discusses the healing power of writing, how telling one's story was the only thing besides massage that helped Holocaust survivors.

Hypergraphists cover surfaces with tiny letters, cryptic messages from our darkest internal catacombs. My friend, memoirist Samantha Dunn, told me she saw Joyce Carol Oates crawling spider-like into her limo after an event, reaching for her laptop and hunkering down over it to spin her web as the driver pulled away. How could Oates have written *Blonde* for instance—her masterpiece novel about Marilyn Monroe, told in a rule-breaking plethora of perspectives— without such obsessive outpourings?

For Alice Flaherty, the hypergraphia began with stillborn twins. Seemingly nonsensical scrawlings of grief eventually became *The Midnight Disease*. In the same way, I've written to transform pain, to save my mind from its incessant loopings, to save my life.

IN THIS BOOK, I'll show you how to **use your pain**, or just daily stress, to **feed your art**; how to **tune into the wisdom** of that inner **muse** and **mentor**; **ignore your critic** until the time is right; **create order** from chaos; **live simply** but expressively; fructify; **persevere**; trust; **face your shadow**; find **magic**; **create art for those you love** rather than as a commodity for a larger, faceless and judgmental audience; and maybe even **change the world**! I'll show you that if you have the burning life-or-death desire, or even the curious wish, to express yourself creatively, it *is* possible.

You can do it. And I can help.

Besides using anecdotes from my life and examples from the work of other writers, I'll give you alternating chapters of writing exercises based on a series of twelve interrelated questions that I've developed over three decades, and that can be applied to fiction, memoir, screenplays, and even poetry.

Life might be hard, but art? This we can do. Together.

1

ECHO
—— Find a Mentor

M Y FATHER WAS A MENTOR, NOT A HEROIN ADDICT.
I say this because my father, Irving Alexander Block,
like the father of my most well-known fictional character
Weetzie, *was* a lovable, playful, highly creative charmer who
worked as a screenwriter, art director, and special effects
man. But Weetzie's father died of an overdose, dreaming of
poppies, and my father couldn't even manage a glass of red
wine or a hit of a joint without falling asleep. Even coffee was
soon replaced by a bitter, granular caffeine-free substitute
with an unappetizing name! If he was addicted to anything,
it might have been bread and chocolate, and painting. And
my mother, whom he painted obsessively.

His oils and watercolors didn't just depict the pink ama-
ryllis lilies and purple and white irises; the lemons, avocados,

plums, and peaches that my mother grew in her garden; the musical instruments, candlesticks, ceramic bowls, and ancient iridescent Egyptian tear catchers that she arranged for him. These paintings were, I think, more portraits of his muse-wife.

He had studied fine art in New York and worked in the tradition of masters like Zurbaran and Morandi; 1970s celebrities such as the famed cinematographer Haskell Wexler, the football player turned actor/poet Bernie Casey, and the throaty-voiced actress Lee Grant bought his paintings from a chic, mid-century modern gallery on La Cienega Boulevard, and my dad's work hung in the Hirshhorn Museum. The paint is richly textured, complexly layered, and, even years after its initial application, seems to glow from within.

To supplement the money he made as a painter, my father worked for years as a professor of art history and film, and his hippy students were always coming over for dinners my mother made—vegetarian lasagna; chile rellenos; brisket with sweet potatoes, carrots, and raisins; salmon steaks with dill and sour cream. We ate at a long picnic-style scarred-oak, candle-wax-coated table in a room embellished with wooden carvings out of an Eastern European fairy tale.

My father had bought the house, with the pink oleander bushes in front and the eucalyptus trees in back, at the Valley-side base of Laurel Canyon, with cash; he never owned a credit card. This was the rather grounded but bohemian world where I grew up and learned to be an artist under my father's tutelage.

MY DAD DIDN'T have a heroin problem—he was stable and responsible—but, like many of the fathers in my books, he did have a dark side.

Before he met my mother, my father traveled; maybe he was looking for her, although they both ended up in Hollywood (even, perhaps, side by side eating ice cream sundaes at Schwab's Pharmacy where Lana Turner had been discovered, though my mother was only a little girl at the time).

On a trip to Mexico, as my father walked along the crowded streets, something fell out of the paper bag he carried and began to roll away. A human skull. He needed it for a model, to sketch, to understand the shape beneath the skin, perhaps to help him understand his own mortality. The passersby looked bewildered as he attempted to grab the thing and put it back in the bag. I often think of this image as symbolic of at least one part of my father: blackly comic, at the mercy of death and art.

He always seemed acutely conscious of his own temporal nature and this awareness somehow touched me by osmosis; even when he was in perfect health, I often worried about his impending death. In third grade, I asked a classmate if she ever felt this way about her own father, who was a few years older than some of the other dads, though younger than mine. Her bewildered response made me realize that my fears were not "normal," but it didn't dispel them. After all, my father was twenty-two years my mother's senior, easily old enough to be her parent and my grandfather.

On Halloween, he created a "haunted house" in his studio. The infamous skull was part of the tableau, along with a plastic skeleton that he used in his anatomy class, a plaster model of an arm and hand, and a transparent cherub mask that he'd found in a warehouse of old movie props where he went, in spite of my mother's qualms, to sketch nude models once a week.

Other skeletons shadow-danced in my father's closet. For example, no one in our home ever mentioned his first wife, a woman with, oddly, a name similar to mine and, less oddly, to his dead mother's—a woman who, I managed to discover, had been dark-haired like me, beautiful like my mom, and quite mad.

One of the two pictures I have of him as a child shows my father wearing frilly white pants and scowling in the shadow of a stern woman in a white Victorian dress. His mother, Frida, or "Fanny," died of tuberculosis soon after. Though three loving, blue-eyed, seamstress sisters raised him (the other picture shows a laughing, curly-haired elf in a white nightgown, clearly the object of the sister-photographer's great affection), my father never fully recovered from his mother's death, and his severe father, owl-eyed and unsmiling in *his* photographs, provided an angry and discouraging foil for a budding, brooding young artist.

> My father carried on the traditions of his heritage by reading prayers and poetry.

My father rarely mentioned his early career in the studios, except to tell me that *Forbidden Planet*, the 1956 sci-fi classic he co-wrote with partner Allen Adler, was based on Shakespeare's *The Tempest*; that he traveled to Paris to work in the art department on an animated puppet version of *Alice in Wonderland*; and that my father once saw Marilyn Monroe on a set.

The reason for all this reticence? My father became a victim of McCarthyism, based on his attendance at socialist meetings. (He would later insist on public medicine and school for me, though I longed to attend the private school where boys grew their hair long and wore tie-dye, girls eschewed makeup, and yearbook pictures weren't studio portraits but casual arty snapshots of kids lounging on the lawn.) His name was removed from many of his projects, and, after being lauded by the likes of George Lucas—who said *Forbidden Planet* had a huge influence on his work—only reinstated years later.

World events affected my father profoundly. When Robert Kennedy was shot, my dad heard it on the radio while painting a still life. He slapped a streak of black across the canvas, obscuring the flowers underneath. The news depressed him but he watched it every night, lying in the dark staring at the black and white storm on the TV screen. I often joined him, just to be close, but his rigid posture and impassive face, that had been so cheerful at breakfast, worried me. Was he internalizing, in some way, all the pain he witnessed?

Other aspects of my father's personality mitigated his dark nature: his great warmth and humor.

Yes, he had me walk through his haunted studio, but he also dressed up as Santa Claus, in red pajamas and with a beard made of shaving cream, and the Easter Bunny, in white pajamas and a pillowcase mask with ears. One picture of

Easter-Irving shows him poised on our backyard hillside, among the passion flower vines with their seedy fruits, holding a basket of strawberry-sized wooden rabbits, chicks made of silk tassels, hand-dyed eggs, and fresh daffodils, that had been delivered to our doorstep by our Viennese friends Hans and Lisl Hacker who had escaped Nazi-occupied Europe and lived in a house in the Hollywood Hills full of bags of this Easter paraphernalia and boxes of good luck pigs that they set out every New Year's Eve. My father looks uncannily lagomorphic emerging from the morning mist.

Born Jewish, he also carried on the traditions of his heritage by reading prayers and poetry at holiday dinners and sneaking sips of wine on Passover to make me think that the angel Elijah had visited. (I began resting one fingertip on the goblet in order to catch my father in the act and he soon, to my dismay, gave up this practice.)

He loved almost all food, especially breads and cakes, and anything my mother made, but also the tiny herrings and sweet chicken wings from the Swedish smorgasbord; buttered corn tortillas and huge plates of beans and rice at El Cholo, where the waitresses wore full-length crinolines under their dresses; platters of pasta—which he insisted on passing around the table so everyone could have a taste—from Little Joe's in the Chinatown district; and the sticky orange rolls from the Tick Tock Tea Room with cuckoo clocks popping out from the walls. Food, for him, was magic. He even relished the little trays of prepackaged meals that airlines used to provide (especially the cardboard-stiff chocolate brownies) because, he told me, "It's a miracle to eat 40,000 feet up in the sky!"

One night there was a dinner party at the home of the Swiss abstract expressionist Hans Burkhardt, a protégé of Arshile Gorky. While my father hid his dark side by painting fruits, flowers, and the women who resembled them, Hans used actual human bones in his compositions but appeared as merry as an elf with his snowy hair, cherry cheeks, and Nutcracker features. Hans's wife, Thordis, a very proper, pinch-lipped woman, a few feet taller than her husband and an early advocate of whole wheat bread, nutritional yeast, and other "health foods," served us aspic, a foodstuff I'd never seen before. It horrified me, and my father came to my aid, lifting the slab of jelly with his fork and knife and trying to surreptitiously navigate it across to his plate, when it splatted onto the white linen tablecloth, jiggling meatily for all to see.

Another equally embarrassing moment: He took my mother and me to the Griffith Observatory and told us to watch for him on the camera obscura. He went outside and staggered along in a state of fake drunkenness, exclusively for our benefit.

My father's antics might have mortified me at times, but his students loved him. Once, while walking on the campus of the college where he taught, two seven-foot-tall Black, afroed basketball players passed my dad, one on either side and one said, in a voice my father loved to imitate: "Well hello there, Mr. Ein-stein!" With his unruly gray hair, glasses, tweeds, and turtlenecks, he truly did resemble the genius he admired.

By far the best story about my father, though—the one that most encapsulates his mentoring abilities—came during a final exam. One of his students had said he desperately needed to do well in the class to graduate. On the day of the test, the student developed a nosebleed and continued to fill in the answers, head tilted back, hand over face, while blood spattered across the white paper.

My father came over to him, drew an "A" in the red liquid with his finger, patted the student on the back and sent him home.

This is how I learned to teach.

This is how I learned that artists bleed their work.

MY FATHER MENTORED me even before I was alive.

When I was in utero, my father read Keats and Yeats, Pablo Neruda and Shakespeare's sonnets to my mother and me. He chose my name in part for one of his favorite artists, Piero Della Francesca—whose painting of strangely blank-faced, angelic, lute-playing women hung on our wall.

My father told me *The Odyssey* and other myths as bed-time stories, showed me his collection of art books, took me to the museum every weekend, and drew with me in the evenings. He introduced me to the spectrum of mysteriously named colors in his paint box, the feel of greasy pastels that stained my fingertips, and the application of gold-leaf fila-ments, thin as insect wings.

For my twelfth birthday, my dad ordered a subscription to *The American Poetry Review*, which featured work by Denise

Levertov, Audre Lorde, and Adrienne Rich. When I was six-teen, he illustrated two chapbooks of my poetry and a small press published them on fine marbled paper, tied with pale blue ribbon.

He also cared for me in practical ways. He was our "short order cook," frying eggs and making pancakes shaped like hearts, including tiny ones for my dolls, all the while impersonating a variety of silly accents. Even during his most successful years as a painter, he went to work five days a week, causing me to beg him, "Take off your coat and don't go to the college." He dressed wounds and removed splinters with cool, capable, tapered hands. (I remember being wrung with jealousy when he tweezed a splinter out of a neighbor girl's finger.)

{ This is how I learned that artists bleed their work. }

The day he died he walked to the bank to put money in my account and left my mother with enough resources to support her for the rest of her life.

No one could have had a better creative mentor or caretaker.

But.

Like any human, my father had his dark tendencies, his skeletons. He wasn't perfect, and, like most parents, he wasn't able to fulfill all of his child's deep needs.

A therapist once told me this story of a man and his daughter: As she walked down a staircase toward him at a party in their home, the man said, in front of the gathered crowd, "Here comes the most beautiful girl in the world."

This made me weep as I envisioned the smiling father with eyes only for his child, the seen daughter shining in the beam of his light. I had never heard those words.

"That's what a father is supposed to tell his daughter," the therapist said. "Not just that she's a good storyteller."

Even when I was twelve, with china teacup skin and honeyshine hair, when I might have believed him, he never shouted, "You are a beautiful girl!"

My father called me a writer.

He acknowledged me as a creative person, like himself, which I loved. But not as an attractive and worthy female, which hurt.

I also intuited early on that the role of muse was what made a girl into a real woman and there was only room for one muse in our house—my mother, a larger-than-life Demeter earth goddess, her basket overflowing with fresh baked bread, wild roses, and home-grown carrots and tomatoes still dusted with earth.

She wrote poetry herself, played the lute, danced, read me fairy tales, took me to the library every week to check out the maximum amount of books, and, when I began writing, helped me edit my stories. But she had given up her own dreams as a dancer and writer to cook and care for her husband and children, to assemble the still lifes my father painted, and to pose for him in flowing homemade dresses, her inlaid mahogany lute in her lap, while I remained invisible, underground: chthonic Persephone lost in the darkness.

Hades didn't capture me and pull me down with him. I went searching there for him. I've been searching all these years.

This invisibility, this search for Hades, gave me a whole lot to write about. And the ability to use pain as a source of inspiration? Another lesson from my father. It might even have ultimately been more important than his direct encouragement.

In my book about a young woman searching for her identity through her relationships, a skeleton named Mister Bones, fastened onto her dead artist father's canvas, then gobbed with paint, tells her, " . . . *Echo is not meant to be seen. She is meant to see.*"

IF YOU DON'T have a parent-mentor, teachers can be instrumental in helping form a budding artist's sensibilities. In first grade, Miss Atlas, a Twiggy lookalike with her teased blond beehive, long fake lashes, and skinny legs enhanced by micro minis and platform shoes, designated me the "class poet." I remember how she smelled of the peach-boxed, dove-bottled Chloe perfume and the cigarettes that huskied her voice when all my female classmates and I clamored around to hold her hands with the dangerous nails.

Miss Atlas gave me nothing but solace. She printed out a poem I'd written, "The Flyaway Kite," and posted it on the wall:

> *I fly in the blue of the flowery morn*
> *I fly through blossoming trees,*
> *I fly in a deep pink sunset*
> *past butterflies and bees*

I was lost in the wind on a starry night, from the hands
   of a little boy,
I know it was mean to fly away
but I am not a regular toy
I must fly, I must fly, I must be free!
Nothing at all can bother me.

In fourth grade, Mrs. Eisenmann, the first openly masculine woman I'd ever known well, let me write, direct, produce, and perform in a play called *Help*, where a demon doll bled from its eyes!

Mrs. Rosenthal, my sixth-grade teacher with a Mary Tyler Moore grin, taught us about the Renaissance, had us write poems based on Edna St. Vincent Millay's "Renascence," let me play a witch in *Macbeth*, and championed my writing for years.

Some of my teacher-mentors taught me not by nurturing but by challenging, even with harsh treatment. A ballet teacher I studied with as an adult would hook my leg with his cane and pull until it hurt. One evening, in that high-ceilinged, talcum-and-steel-wool-scented studio on the east end of Pico Boulevard, where I struggled to keep up beside my much more experienced and younger peers, the Polish master, with his severe accent and bulging calves, declared, "Francesca, you do not feel comfortable in your own body!"

How true. And how horrid to hear it spoken aloud.

I later studied with another instructor, one who encouraged me, more kindly, to grow as a dancer. And I did—so much that I was invited to dance with her at Highways, the legendary art space off Olympic, where I'd seen Phranc the lesbian punk folk singer perform years before. The Highways event gave me my first and only opportunity to live out—or at least stumble through—my childhood dream of being a dancer (after which I promptly "retired").

Through these teacher-mentors, I learned more than how to move and dance. I learned to work with my body in spite of my frustrations with it, to stay calm in the face of judgment, and to push myself for my own satisfaction rather than the approval of others.

FRIENDS AND COLLEAGUES **can also be instrumental in supporting and nurturing you.**

The important thing is to be careful about who you choose to let into this part of your life. Toxic friends and lovers, out of envy, fear, or insensitivity, might not have your best interests at heart. Writer Mary Pauline Lowry says: "This is something that takes lots of intuition, but it's good to trust your gut on who is 'safe' and redirect quickly if you show to someone who gives a brutal read. Constructive feedback is so different from mean/cruel feedback!"

If you're short on actual people to share your art with, **there will always be books to inspire, guide, and comfort you.** My Secret Man carries a strap-ripping stack around in his backpack wherever he goes and has worked at bookstores for years in order to be as close to as much reading material as possible. As a lonely child, books companioned him, and as an adult they taught him about the world around him, and about the world inside.

Therapists can also offer profound support, but it isn't easy to find the right one. Perhaps this search is as difficult as finding a life partner. There are many imposters (in both areas).

One therapist I met told me I'd be happier if I were more beautiful. She'd brought me into her gated community condo, where I lay on her bed while she sat on an upholstered Marimekko-print chair beside me. "What don't you like? Your hair? Your eyes? Your smile? Your nose? Aha! I know a plastic surgeon. I'm considering using him myself. But I'll see how he does on you. Also, he's very handsome. And I think he's single!"

A young, sloe-eyed therapist I saw in college suggested I wear *less* makeup. Then he nodded off while I was telling him about my dying father.

Another therapist told me, "Never look at yourself in the rearview mirror of your car. You'll see all the worst things," and, "You know, Francesca, neither of us are the best-looking women in the world."

Then finally, finally I found Sofia. Interesting that she had been a painter and a teacher like my dad. She turned to psychotherapy at first as a way to help her art students, one of whom decided he wanted to kill an animal as part of his thesis project. Like my dad, she also shared a penchant for Carl Jung; flight-suggesting Persian carpets replete with birds and pomegranates; and the anthropomorphizing of dogs.

Sofia explained *attachment theory*, the idea that if we don't form a strong, secure bond of unconditional acceptance with a caregiver as a child (a bond—developed through eye contact, voice contact, skin contact, and consistency of action and tone—that actually changes the developing brain), we can try to seek it through a therapist. Eventually we can begin to internalize what we might not have gotten from the parent, or what we might have gotten in a broken way. She explained the difference between the child who cries when her parent leaves her with a responsible but unfamiliar adult and then recovers and plays, the child who cries and never recovers until the parent returns, and the child who is unmoved.

I think of myself, even as old as thirteen, lying awake in the dark at slumber parties, suffocated with fear. Like a baby alone in a dark hospital room, hooked up to intravenous fluids through incisions in her ankles. Sofia also explained that insecure attachments foster more of the same, throughout a person's lifetime. My parents were certainly there for me, but their own attachments were insecure, and they passed the anxiety on.

{ The people we love are not perfect. Neither are our mentors. }

As much as my dad gave me, his fears affected my self-esteem.

I recently showed Sofia a picture of my parents and me at age twelve. My dad with his big glasses and prominent nose smiles goofily; his hands are in motion; his hair is a halo of silver light. My blond mother, with her slim-chiseled symmetrical features, appears frozen and perfect. I look solemn and somewhat bewildered. "I feel more like my dad's little twin," I said. "Not like my mom at all."

"You are a mirror image of your mom now," Sofia observed, though I still don't see it. "And your dad is hugging you and laughing in this picture."

Maybe my father—my original mentor—valued me as more than just a good writer, an artist for him to guide. But this realization would take years to set in. And by not believing it, I handily fed my childhood wound. Perhaps every artist needs to face his in order to create. No matter how painful the process.

The people we love are not perfect. Neither are our mentors. No one is.

But even our mentors' "flaws" can be inspiration for our art. We must seek help from the best and brightest around us, and embrace their gifts when they arrive.

THE 12 QUESTIONS: GIFTS AND FLAWS

Question #1: What is your character's gift?
Question #2: What is your character's flaw?

Gifts

In order for the reader to care about a protagonist, she must have, among other things, a special **gift**. Lisa Cron, author of *Wired for Story: The Writer's Guide to Using Brain Science to Hook Readers from the Very First Sentence*, says that the survivalist aspect of storytelling can only be fully realized if the reader deeply identifies with the main character and her predicament.

Often, beginning writers complete whole first drafts and don't know what is special (in both positive *and* negative ways) about their main characters. Sometimes, in the case of the "gift," this is because many novels are autobiographical, and most of us don't really value or even see our own best qualities. Our friends do, and it helps to ask them.

Whether or not they are autobiographical, characters usually do have a special gift, even in a rough first draft, though it may not be developed or externalized enough in the early stages. In later drafts, imagine how you might demonstrate the character's gift in both overt and subtle ways. If your character is intelligent, you can *tell* your reader she is brilliant, but your story will be richer if you *show* your character's genius through her actions. For example, can your character apply her skills of logic to solve a problem, even if that problem isn't central to the plot?

In fantasy, paranormal, magical realism, speculative, and science fiction, gifts can be externalized in dramatic ways. A character can have visions, telepathy, telekinetic abilities, or other superpowers. In realistic fiction, the writer must show a special gift in the context of everyday life, and through action. It's important that the gift can be demonstrated actively, not just through how the character perceives the world but in how he interacts in the world. The character may not be aware of his gift (this may make him someone even more likeable), but the writer and reader should be acutely aware.

A quieter version of a gift is a **simple skill**. A simple skill can also be important to the definition of a character. As Stephen King says in *On Writing*, people love to read about work. A character with a special, practical work skill—that is shown in realistic detail through the course of the book—reads as sympathetic and compelling.

HERE ARE A few examples of gifts from some classic novels:

In Harper Lee's *To Kill a Mockingbird*, Scout's gift is her innocence, which allows her to keep her faith in humanity.

In F. Scott Fitzgerald's *The Great Gatsby*, Gatsby's gift is his drive to succeed.

Charlotte Bronte bestows Jane Eyre with the gifts of both passion and reason.

In Vladimir Nabokov's *Lolita*, Humbert's gift is his crafty determination.

Maria, the actress protagonist in Joan Didion's *Play It As It Lays*, is gifted with perseverance: She is a survivor who keeps playing the game, keeps driving the LA highways, even if she hasn't found meaning yet.

Flaws

Another way to help a reader identify with a protagonist (and thereby gain more life-enhancing insight from the story) is to show that character's humanity through her **flaws**. Flaws also get a character into trouble, which satisfies the reader's need for story. Don't worry about making your characters "too flawed" as long as they are complex and interesting. Perhaps the worst thing you can do is bore your reader.

> Like our characters, our strengths and our weaknesses are what make us unique.

THE BEST CHARACTER **gifts are those that can appear as strong flaws when taken to the negative extreme.** For example, the extreme negative of emotional strength can be psychic numbness, and the extreme negative of loving can be smothering.

> In *To Kill a Mockingbird*, Scout's flaws are her stubbornness and pride, and also her naïveté, which is the negative extreme of innocence.
>
> In *The Great Gatsby*, Gatsby's ambition, taken to the extreme, destroys him.
>
> Jane Eyre can be impetuous, and sometimes she also quashes her passion with excessive reason and self-denial.
>
> In Emily Brontë's *Wuthering Heights*, Heathcliff is passionate about Catherine, but this desire, when corrupted, becomes cruelty.
>
> In *Lolita*, Humbert's passion is channeled into an unhealthy obsession with a child.
>
> Maria in *Play It As It Lays* has shut down, turning passive and nihilistic.

As writers, our gifts can also be our flaws and vice versa. For example, a very lyrical, poetic novelist may have trouble moving the plot forward as he indulges in the pleasures of imagery, and a very plot-driven writer may neglect the nuances of language.

The key is knowing our writerly gifts and flaws, developing the former and improving upon the latter, while being aware that—like our characters—our strengths and our weaknesses are what make us unique.

2

DANGEROUS ANGELS
—— Find a Muse

A S AN ARTIST LIKE MY FATHER, RATHER THAN A MUSE
like my mother, I needed a source of inspiration.

At an early age, I adopted a male persona and wrote love
poems to a blond goddess who resembled my mom. When
my parents looked puzzled, I realized I had to seek my muse
elsewhere. But I had also learned that this elusive creature
was more than just a creative guide. In my father's case, she
was the beloved, quick to share an all-encompassing smile
that twinkled with fillings I saw as further expression of her
beauty—her "golden beads."

Since the evening they met at a classical music concert
in the late 1950s in LA, they had never spent a single night
apart (except when he hesitated to marry her, thinking he
was too old, and she put my brother, Zack, her son from her

first marriage, into her VW Bug with stuffing exploding from the seats, and drove up to Berkeley to get her master's in English; my father followed her, brought her home, and married her on the spot). They held hands wherever they went. When my father died my mother told me she wanted to go, too.

Besides the emphasis on creativity, my parents conveyed a tacit message that without an almost preternatural love relationship, I might never be happy, even if I became a successful artist. For that, too, I needed someone outside of myself. A true love, like my parents had both found.

So the search for a muse, and beloved, began.

But it's hard enough to find even one of these things, let alone someone who embodies them both.

At ten, watching television with seventeen-year-old Zack. My parents were out on a date, either seeing a film by Woody Allen, Bergman, or Bertolucci; eating *coq au vin* at an intimate French restaurant on Ventura Boulevard; or at a dinner party with my father's colleagues from the college where he taught.

Sometimes during those nights my brother fell asleep before I did, and my parents came home to find me sitting bolt upright staring at the screen. That night my brother stayed awake, as entranced as I; on *Midnight Special* a slender man with a dark beard played his guitar and sang.

White button shirt, blue jeans; I think he was barefoot. He had a slightly throaty but very sweet voice and even through the black-and-white screen I could feel the golden radiance shining off his Greek and Swedish skin. I could smell the heady redolence of patchouli, the scent of record shops and hippy boutiques like the one my mother took me to, bins collaged with photos of bare-breasted girls. The man sang about peace. His voice rumbled through my body like a distant locomotive.

A few months later, Zack and his girlfriend took me to see Cat Stevens at The Forum. I wore suede platform sandals, yellow Ditto's jeans, a rainbow-striped sleeveless sweater with rhinestones sprinkled over it, and a denim jacket that my mom and I had decorated with more rhinestones, using a small gun. I sat on the edge of the seat, literally perched there so that the plastic made imprints on the back of my thighs, and watched the man illuminated in a small spotlight; tears poured off of me like sweat.

No one loved Cat Stevens like I did. Like a betrothed. How could they? I lay on my parents' couch, listening to the songs over and over again, wanting to crawl into the album covers. Those watercolors of strange little boys in orange top hats, feeding fish bones to cats. Chocolate Buddhas wrapped in gold foil. Photographs of that lithe, feline god. My favorite song: "Oh Very Young." He was singing to me. Singing about the thing no one else understood—the fear that my father, who was older than anyone else's dad, would not last forever, that my own death was also imminent, and that all I could do in the face of it was carry the words of love . . . and dance.

My father shone a small desk lamp as a spotlight as I flung myself around my living room in a black leotard while Cat Stevens sang. I was seen—briefly. Then I developed breasts and hips and my father looked away.

I had one wish at that age, besides world peace and for my father to live to see me into adulthood. I wanted to come face to face with my idol, my muse.

When my parents took me to London in 1972, between visits to the National Gallery, the Victoria and Albert, flea markets, and a toy store filled with gingerbread-style doll-houses and bisque and Penny Wooden dolls, I made my mother help me search for the Greek restaurant Cat Stevens's parents purportedly owned. As if we'd find him slinking through the deserted, foggy night streets. I wore tiny purple suede, lace-up gillies my parents bought me on Kings Road where the "birds" sported huge floppy hats, bell bottoms, and modly colored platform shoes. My mother and I walked up and down in the dark; that was how much she indulged me. Somehow we would find my beloved muse in his snakeskin pants.

No such luck. Instead, I wrote love poems and short stories to him. I sent one of the poems but it was returned with a black and white photo of Cat glancing away from the camera. His record company had rejected my small offering, and I couldn't even see his eyes in the picture, let alone be seen, and recognized, by him.

THEN, SEVEN YEARS later, my wish came true.

My friend Dirk and I stopped his two-tone 1955 Pontiac convertible at McNatural's on the Sunset Strip for a vegetarian lunch. We needed healthy food after staying up all night at a Weirdos and Oingo Boingo show at the Whisky, drinking the expensive chardonnay Dirk had stolen from his mother's cellar and eating bean, cheese, hotdog, and pastrami burritos at Oki Dog's, the destination for after-hours punk kids, then on Santa Monica Boulevard.

Dirk's Mohawk still stood pristine after a night of slamming in a pit; he smelled of Aquanet and alcohol, had huge black-and-white leopard-print Doc Marten creepers from Poseur on his feet. I wore an old pink satin prom dress and the black leather steel-toed engineer boots I'd found at St. Vincent de Paul thrift store for $15. A girl with a Mohawk had hacked off my hair at a barbershop called Head Hunter's in the San Fernando Valley.

No one else in the cool, quiet restaurant except us, and one man. He wore a peach tunic that gilded his tawny skin. Masses of black curls, a dark beard, the most sensual lips; even his nose, sensual. Uncanny eyes.

They stared into mine, deep and darkly, as if acknowledging not only my physical presence but the very depths of my soul. Masculine strength, love, wisdom, and enlightenment blazed before me . . . and then I looked away, afraid of petrification. I was too young, too uncertain, to face the idealized manifestation of my animus embodied in this man.

Dirk and I had spotted Tina Turner getting out of a car along the strip, and Stevie Wonder bobbing his head in a limousine, but I refused to believe that the man sitting before me now, looking directly into my eyes, was actually my idol.

Then, the next day in the *Times*, there appeared an article about how Yusef Islam, formerly known as Cat Stevens, had come to town to sell his collection of gold records.

Somehow, though I hadn't been able to acknowledge it at the time, he had seen my true self. This really happened: The muse I had searched for, longed for, had appeared as if summoned by a genie from a magic lamp.

Did he stare into everyone's eyes? Was he trying to tell me something? Comfort me? (I'd read he'd been abused as a child. His father locked him in a closet. Beat him. "Father and Son.") Correct my ways? (He'd experimented with drugs and sex. "Wild World.") Was he trying to bring me back into my body? I had left it and would continue to do so many times in my life. It wasn't where I wanted to be. When I wrote my poems and little stories dedicated to the muses, daughters of the sky god, Zeus, and Mnemosyne, goddess of memory, I could escape for at least a short time, which felt good, but also risky. What if I never came back to myself?

> My own death was imminent and all I could do in the face of it was carry the words of love.

Was Cat Stevens simply, like any good muse, trying to inspire me?

I continued to seek the muse after that encounter and my subsequent disillusionment with him. But until I'd found myself, every relationship, even the sweetest, had the potential for self-annihilation.

IN SEPTEMBER 1981, my platinum-Mohawked friend, Lise, and I were sitting on the floor of the ballroom in San Francisco where X was about to play. I wore an ecru and pale blue lace 1950s prom dress, pointed turquoise satin pumps, and my vintage rhinestone jewelry, a pink rhinestone cat collar around my wrist. I pointed at a boy I recognized from the UC Berkeley dorm cafeteria, and said to Lise, "Him."

"What about him?" she asked.

"He's my future boyfriend," I declared. After all, I needed someone to write about in my poetry class!

I went over and introduced myself. In spite of my overall lack of confidence at the time, I somehow believed I could get a boyfriend like an "A" in school, pluck him like one of the stories floating around in my head. I was also drunk.

"Hi, Bowie," I said. He had the same slim body and fair complexion. Even the same small, delicate, almost skeletal features. My features felt too big, almost masculine, in comparison.

"It's Thorn. And I prefer the Velvet Underground."

Thorn wore eyeliner and a short-sleeved button-down cotton shirt, like Bowie in the "Be My Wife" video, a beaten-up brown leather jacket, jeans and Converse. This young man's body looked so willowy that I wanted to will myself thinner so as not to overwhelm him.

On stage, Exene bent at the waist like a broken doll, leaned in to wail with John Doe. Their voices pure punk-rock-sex.

"I want to write prose that makes people feel like this," I told Thorn. "Visceral. To make you shake and sweat. Like music does."

After the concert, we took the train back to campus together, and we were a couple by morning.

It was all so easy. How could it have been so easy?

Muffledly fucking in the dorm rooms so we didn't wake my drunk roommate; running together through Strawberry Canyon; going to the Mabuhay Gardens and the Berkeley Square and the Fillmore to hear The Dead Kennedys and Black Flag and New Order and Echo and the Bunnymen; listening to Thorn's Velvet Underground and Traffic albums; eating cheap soup and half sandwiches on whole wheat bread at the Soup Kitchen; reading to each other as we drank glass goblets of coffee in the lugubrious dim of Café Roma, or Italian sodas in the sunshine at Intermezzo, where Thorn admired the light catching the multicolored rhinestones studding my ears.

We shot a punk version of a scene from *A Midsummer Night's Dream* for my Shakespeare in Film class. I, the fairy wearing vintage lace, frolicked around Thorn, Puck in his leather jacket, who flirted back shyly with me, in a garden made of stone. We wrote poems to each other, two of which were published, side by side, in a UC Berkeley literary journal.

I lost weight and cut my hair and dressed like a boy in black jeans, torn T-shirts, and my steel-toed boots, stomping around Polk Street with Thorn, drinking shiny blue cocktails at Hamburger Mary's while Roxy Music's "Slave to Love" played on the jukebox, or at the club with the dried-ice-filled swimming pool. Part of me wanted to be a man who loved men, as if that could save me from the fecund burden of my female body, so that I could dance at the Stud and go home with a boy in eyeliner and chains. Fuck him, have him fuck me back.

Once I said to Thorn, "If I were a boy, I'd be you."

"No," he said. "You'd be much wilder."

Even the Bay Area spring is melancholy, when the fruit trees blossom and the air smells sweet. I wanted to eat flowers, stuff my face with them. I couldn't get warm. But Thorn held me in our glass room, tried to heat my body as best he could.

I was the one who ruined things, starved myself away to nothing, trying to disappear.

Nothing glamorous about it. My hair sprouted grays, my ass ached on the wooden seats of lecture halls, I destroyed my gums, my bones.

I woke up crying one night and Thorn asked me what was wrong.

"I'm hungry," I said, thinking of the shredded wheat and nonfat milk in the filthy kitchen downstairs.

"Just eat." He turned away on our tiny futon that smelled of sweet straw in the glass porch room in the old South Berkeley house. The bare-branched plum tree scratched its fingernails against the window, shredding our already frayed nerves with the sound.

How could I explain I couldn't just eat? It made no sense. I didn't understand. A house full of women with eating disorders and a couple of wan boyfriends. Thorn and I had to walk over people in bedrolls to get to our room. They looked dead. Body bags.

One day, I hiked up the hill to the medical center because I wasn't getting my period. Was I pregnant?

I wasn't.

"You're pre-anorexic," the nurse said.

She offered no treatment.

I EXPERIENCED MORE pain when John and Exene split up than when I had to drop out of school and leave Thorn, because by then the anorexia ("pre" or not, I'd rapidly lost over twenty pounds) had transformed me into a heartless fae who could feel almost nothing. My father, still under treatment for cancer, drove with my mother to pick me up.

Thorn, standing in front of that big wooden house with the glass room where we shivered in our sleep, hugged me. I felt his scapula winging through his shirt. He put something in my hand. A tiny white plastic dove. My parents and I loaded my few things into the Volvo, already coated with the dirt of I-5, and drove away.

I stared out at the oleanders along the freeway and tried not to think of Thorn. My father stopped at Dairy Queen and I ate a soft serve ice cream though I hadn't tasted sugar or fat in months. The vanilla swirling against my tongue recalled Christina Rossetti's goblin fruit. I went back to my parents' home in the valley and slept and slept, waking only briefly to write fragments of eldritch poetry.

No one ever properly treated me for anorexia, but those poems are part of how I recovered. So were the short stories I wrote about my muse Thorn, as I'd predicted when I met him. They would later win me a UC Berkeley creative writing award, but at the time I just wanted the man who had inspired them. It was too late. I was no longer a human girl but a creature, ethereal, half-crazed, and starving in every way.

THE SUMMER AFTER I returned from Berkeley I got a job at Aphrodite's store on Melrose, where I'd worked briefly before I left for college. My friends and I had stumbled through Aphrodite's door looking for prom dresses to find Aphrodite herself sitting in front of a turquoise vinyl curtain sewing, her eyes glazed with dreams of dresses she'd soon make; beside her, severed white gardenia heads floated in a bowl. The store didn't have air conditioning and the air sweltered, the vinyl curtain dripped with condensation.

"You should come work for me one day," she said. So I did.

While I was away at Berkeley, Aphrodite had redecorated her place in a Gaudi-esque style with fluid columns inlaid with bits of broken pottery. The jade-green stone floor made the salesgirls' backs hurt and wore our kitten heels down to the nails inside.

A mannequin stood in the window. I dressed her up in clothing made from a patchwork of antique, embroidered, and hand-painted silk kimonos (think pink peonies threaded with metallic gold, nacreous seascapes and watercolor cherry blossoms), wrote out her story on poster board in Aphrodite's window, and created little scenarios, including a Valentine's Day display: red and silver glitter hearts inscribed with the names of three people—Smoke, his ex-girlfriend Glinda, and her six-year-old daughter Eden.

I'd met them at a party in Laurel Canyon with my co-worker, Starr, sinister and sweet as one of those floating-headed angels on the then-popular Fiorucci fashion label.

Once, a snobby customer in the store criticized the clothes. Starr marched to the back of the store, turned off Roxy Music, Ryuchi Sakamoto, *Red, Hot, and Blue* or whatever else might have been playing, blasted "Dog Food" by Iggy Pop as loud as it could go, and stomped back in, singing along in a gruff little voice.

Starr, a storm in the form of a girl—her platinum hair teased into a punk bouffant, her eyelids glimmering like mermaid scales. "I need to see Spazz," she told me. "I'm taking you to a party. But first let's go to Venice Beach."

On the boardwalk in Venice, Harry Perry, the roller-skating Sikh with the turban and oracular eyes, zoomed past us, playing electric guitar, white robes streaming. I'd always seen him as some kind of portent of strange things to come.

An elfin clown painted Starr's face and then mine mime-white with pale blue and silver flowers before giving me his phone number. Afterward, Starr drove us to the party in Laurel Canyon, down the road from the mansion where Joni Mitchell lived when she wrote *Ladies of the Canyon*, across from the sprawling, overgrown stone ruins known as Houdini's castle, though it's never been proven if the magician actually resided there.

Sweating the oily flowers off our faces in the sick heat, Starr and I hiked up a steep dirt path in white, pointed leather boots from Let It Rock. The boots would be ruined by the time we hiked back down. The punk rock icon Geza X guarded the door. I had a feeling I'd never be the same.

Spazz, made even taller than his six-feet-something by a huge bleached and gelled Mohawk, pogoed around, shaking his limbs, popping his joints; so otherworldly, except for a face that was just sad and kind. He was about to leave with Toni Basil to dance on the Glass Spiders Japan tour.

Starr loved him. Feverishly. When he left on tour, she pulled out strands of her hair in an alopecia frenzy. She crooned his name. He was her muse and beloved, all she wanted.

I understood. I was intricately aware of my aloneness. In that scene, in the world.

An all-eyes-and-legs six-year-old in a tiara and tutu applied lipstick without a mirror. She knew the exact shape of her mouth already.

"You're good at that," I told her.

"Bowie taught me," she said.

The fairies I'd always looked for in the nether regions of flowers and among the tree roots had manifested as this child, Eden.

I found out later she had been diagnosed with cancer but her mother, Glinda, would not let her daughter die.

A man came up and took Eden's hand, introduced himself as Smoke. Small in stature—not much taller than me—scarred cheekbones that cut my heart, shards-of-blue eyes in an American Spirit haze. He and Eden's mother, Glinda, had been in love before. I hadn't heard him sing yet; when I did it was over.

Smoke sang lead and Glinda sang backup and played keyboards in their band, Pretty Things. All five band members looked alike—maybe it was just the face powder, bleached hair, eyeliner, and lipstick? Starr and I went to see them at Club Lingerie in our artfully hand-torn T-shirts and petticoats. I brought cut out paper stars encrusted with glitter and gave one to Glinda and one to Smoke.

He's the muse. I'm a groupie. Fan. That's all I am.

A nineteen-year-old with a dying father. Not an artist yet, certainly, in spite of my dad's words of encouragement—he was even more ill by this time, retreating further into himself. I needed Smoke, I needed all of them, in order to be someone.

Stirred with desire for Smoke, I called the clown from Venice and invited him over to the apartment building decorated in pink and gray 50s kitsch that I shared with my friend Dirk; the clown made me come. Afterward I froze, couldn't return the favor. What had I gotten myself into? I knew nothing about men's bodies.

"What the fuck?" he said as I fumbled, and then he left.

I didn't blame him.

Searching, searching. Love my heroin. I needed someone to take away the pain.

SMOKE INVITED ME over once. It had been drizzling, a tang of petrichor rose up from the sidewalks. He played *Purple Rain*, its cover a flower storm, in a 1920s pale yellow Beachwood Canyon apartment building under the Hollywood sign. His art on the walls, glitter covering the floor, the scent of tobacco and Nag Champa, doves in the eaves. I was drugged but not on the kind of substances you swallow, smoke, or shoot. My body manufactured them.

"I don't want to get hurt or to hurt anyone," he told me.

I heard whistling when I woke, alone in his bed the next morning with sun white in my eyes, glancing off the glass office buildings in the distance. What was that sound? The Photographer, a thick Israeli man with sunglasses—you never saw his eyes. He'd taken pictures of everyone—Blondie, Madonna, Devo, Lou Reed, Joni. I instinctively feared him. He could smell it on me, I was sure.

Now he stood outside Smoke's window, taunting me with a song by Pretty Things. Why was the Photographer there? He must have been able to smell my fear, I decided, in spite of the morning air, hot with the sharp sweet of white jasmine.

In September I went back to Berkeley. I had to get away from LA. The palm trees were whispering to me through their interpreter, the Santa Anas, convincing me I needed something poisonous that might kill me eventually, so I left.

In the white-walled, wood-floored, almost unfurnished second-floor apartment on Martin Luther King Jr. Way that I shared with a Swiss woman, Pierrette, and her cublike three-year-old son, Raphael, I wrote short stories about Smoke and made collages of his face floating on a black background, shrouded in tulle and sequins, surrounded by stars and the pocket mirrors I'd used as ponds in my childhood dollhouse garden. I painted my female muses Glinda and Eden in watercolors. They all had the same deep-set, pale eyes, watching me from the wall by candlelight.

How did I look lying on my bed in that breast-shaped room with the antique glass light fixture, pink as a nipple, set in the dome? My skin broke out in cysts. I was crying over some Mohawked punk boy I'd just met at a Red Hot Chili Peppers concert, or about my dying father, or about Smoke, whom I kept trying to possess, as both boyfriend and source of inspiration, the way I'd been able to make Thorn mine.

> I wrote my first novel in my head, the way I'd made up stories as a child.

It didn't matter what I was crying about, though; it was all really the same thing. The kind of brutal loneliness that comes only from a loss of self. A deep and omnipresent grief.

Pierrette was pregnant, so she told me I had to find a new place to live. I rented a room in a house near the rose garden in the North Berkeley hills, with a dirty kitchen and four roommates. The only one who (rarely) spoke to me was a tiny Iggy Pop lookalike with a heroin problem.

On my walks to and from campus I wrote my first novel in my head, the way I'd made up stories as a child. Now the storytelling was an attempt to cure the homesickness I felt for my friends and family in Los Angeles, for the city that haunted me, like a muse herself, with a lucent nostalgia.

My book-in-progress was an LA love song, my own private lullaby.

A YOUNG MAN in a white shirt and black jeans practically salsaed up to the table at the macrobiotic restaurant in a little converted bungalow off of Melrose, straight strands of black hair falling charmingly into his lean, angular face.

"What can I get you two lovely ladies?" Angel said, grinning at my mom.

She and I ordered the Moroccan stew with garbanzo beans, yams, and rice.

"You move so gracefully," she said to him. "Are you a dancer?"

"An actor and a drummer," he told us, beating the air rhythmically with his hands. He turned to me. "How about you?"

Without even thinking, I said, "I'm a writer." At that moment, perhaps, like a spell cast, it became true.

A few months later I was sitting at my desk at the art gallery where I worked part time. Almost no one came in anymore, though this space had been a cultural hub in the seventies, with monthly openings where movie stars and art collectors poured out onto the streets. Now the only sound was the pitter-pat of the owner, a former actress, Fifi's little feet as she hurried back and forth across the shiny black floor.

Once, sitting alone in the showroom, I'd seen the dancer Nureyev, with his equine face, peering through the darkened glass at his portrait and then vanishing like a wraith. But this day, some other magic: I received a call from a friend of my father's who had given my manuscript to her publisher: "I have good news. Harper wants to buy your book."

I burst into tears when I realized that my lifelong dream had come to pass. Perhaps, I thought, I had somehow helped manifest it by speaking the words aloud to Angel. *I'm a writer.*

MY LIFE IN BOOKS

Many books, and their writers, have changed my life, but these are the ones I'd most like to transform into human, living teachers if I had a genie lamp to wish upon:

The Animal Family by Randall Jarell: This poetic fable about a solitary hunter and a dark-skinned, blue-eyed, feral mermaid he finds on the beach influenced me by showing me how to create one's own magical, hodge-podge family in a lonely world. I used to scour the dark etchings by Maurice Sendak for signs of the characters but all I could find were a rock formation that vaguely resembled a bear's snout and a picture of waves like scallops of a mermaid's tail. I revisit this book often, and recently read it to Secret Man at night when he had the flu.

The Doll's House by Rumer Godden: This is the story of the Plantaganet family, Mr. Plantaganet; his delicate, flammable wife, Birdy; their baby, Apple; and their friend, Tottie, whose wishes finally come true when their owners give them a doll's house to live in. But after the evil doll Marchpane arrives, disaster ensues. When I read it today I see so many elements that influenced my own work, including the desire for home and family and the dangers that threaten these dreams.

The Metamorphoses by Ovid: My father had taught me all the Greek myths by the time I was a teenager, but this book expressed them with such poetry, and focused on the idea of love as a transformational (healing or destructive) force. I later used it to inspire *Nymph*, my book of erotic short stories.

Nine Stories by J. D. Salinger taught me that prose, like poetry, can be spare and still impactful, perhaps more impactful because of its brevity.

Colette: The profound sensuality of her prose in *Cheri*, about an older woman and her young lover, and the coming-of-age *Claudine* novels, as well as the glamour of Colette's life as a stage performer made me a fan before my twenties.

Charles Baudelaire and Jean Cocteau's poetry collection *Fleurs du Mal*, and the poem, "The Favors of the Moon" in particular, taught me, by the age of thirteen, that darkness, sometimes avoided in my home, only enhances beauty. Cocteau's *Les Enfants Terribles* had the same effect. Those wonderful French!

I used *The Collected Work of Emily Dickinson* for my college thesis paper and, by examining her romance with Death, learned so much about the power of language, rhythm, and imagery, as well as about my own struggles with mortality.

The Cantos by Ezra Pound and the collected poems of both T. S. Eliot and H.D.: I wrote a college thesis paper on the fragment and the void in the work of these three authors. Although Pound's personal life repelled me, I found his use of imagery, incantation, and myth utterly enthralling. H.D. also employed these elements through an ever-expanding feminist perspective that comforted and consoled me with its implicit message: Healing and wholeness are still possible in a broken world.

The raw, brutal emotions and taboo themes confined by visceral language and spare structure in Sylvia Plath's *Ariel* poems made me want to tackle similar material with courage and refinement.

The Collected Plays of Shakespeare: Since my father had used *The Tempest* to inspire *Forbidden Planet*, and my beloved sixth-grade teacher allowed me to play a witch in *Macbeth*, I looked to Shakespeare to learn about . . . everything. The short film I made from *A Midsummer Night's Dream* for my Shakespeare in Film class embedded a fragment from this superhuman writer into my mind.

The Collected Works of William Butler Yeats, *Transformations* by Anne Sexton, *The Bloody Chamber* by Angela Carter, and "Mirror Ball" by Mary Gaitskill: Yeats's belief in the world of fairy gave me permission to consider this a legitimate subject matter. As a fan of the darkest fairy tales, I thrilled to the way Sexton used them to reveal secrets about her personal life. Angela Carter's retellings encouraged me to try the same approach in *The Rose and the Beast*. "Mirror Ball," from the collection *Don't Cry*, uses a fairy tale conceit to metaphorically represent longing and heartache when a boy unwittingly steals an "elfin" girl's soul during casual sex.

I read *The Waves* by Virginia Woolf in college when I was more interested in characterization, language, and imagery than in plot. For the richness of the former elements, perhaps no novel (it might better be called a reverie) is finer. When the one gay male character, Neville, defined the acts of reading and writing poetry, he provided a manifesto of everything I have since learned, through experience, about both (employ "myriad eyes," do not interrupt the flow, be patient and use great care, never avert one's gaze from "fear or horror," do not hesitate to weep or ruthlessly cut away excess) in one deft paragraph.

One Hundred Years of Solitude by Gabriel Garcia Marquez, *The House of the Spirits* by Isabel Allende, and *The Wind-Up Bird Chronicle* by Haruki Murakami offered me an extraordinary recognition of both gritty realism and transcendent magic.

Palm Latitudes and *Lithium for Medea* by Kate Braverman and *L.A. Woman* and *Sex and Rage* by Eve Babitz gave me "permission" to write "indulgently" about what obsessed me in the city I loved.

The Day of the Locust by Nathaniel West, *The Big Sleep* by Raymond Chandler, and *Ask the Dust* by John Fante, all written in 1939, share something besides their publication year: They presented me with unique but related visions of the dark side of Los Angeles.

Last Exit to Brooklyn by Hubert Selby Jr.: "Cubby" Selby, as his friends called him, frequented the gallery on La Cienega where my father showed his art and where I later worked. I was most struck by how the darkness and pre-punk sensibility of the book contrasted with the charming, diminutive man who visited the gallery and who offered me words of support about my own writing. This charm drew the likes of Henry Rollins and Anthony Kiedis to him, while Cubby suffered privately with depression, heroin addiction, and a lung condition.

The controversial *Sexual Personae* by Camille Pagilia, with its study of masculine and feminine expressions in art, provided inspiration for my book about a wild girl in search of her true love who is imprisoned inside a mannequin by an evil artist.

Literary mysteries like *Into the Woods* by Tana French and *The Secret History* by Donna Tartt heavily influenced my first psychological thriller. Both French and Tartt's books are fully grounded in reality but a strange sense of mysticism hovers at the periphery. *The Lovely Bones* by Alice Sebold inspired me in the same way.

House of Leaves by Mark Z. Danielewski is one of the best ghost stories and love stories I've ever read.

In the Cut by Susanna Moore, *Zombie* by Joyce Carol Oates, and *Waiting for Mr. Goodbar* by Judith Rossner all lowered my writerly inhibitions and helped in the execution of my psychosexual thriller.

Blonde by Joyce Carol Oates: Marilyn's story told from many points of view, including first person young Marilyn, first person older Marilyn, third person Marilyn, third person Marilyn's mother, third person Marilyn's friends, collective first person plural "we" of her classmates and fans, etc. These different points of view paint a picture of a fragmented character that everyone sees in a different way.

Never have I wanted to write nonfiction more than after reading *Just Kids* by Patti Smith, a memoir about Patti's life in New York with her photographer muse and beloved, Robert Mapplethorpe. As a super fan of both of them, and of the 1970s Manhattan art scene in general, I knew I would love the book, but it stands on its own for the beauty of its writing and for the emotionality that had me bawling by the end. When my friend Mermaid took me to see Patti interviewed by Jonathan Lethem at the Orpheum, Patti told the audience that her definition of success is not how much money you make or how many friends you have. "All that matters is the canon of work and how it transforms other people."

Diane Arbus: A Biography by Patricia Bosworth and *The Secret Life of The Lonely Doll: The Search for Dare Wright* by Jean Nathan let me see into the lives of artists who shared creativity with the world but struggled with their own private anguish.

Never Let Me Go by Kazuo Ishiguro taught me the beauty of starting with quiet realism and then breaking a reader's heart into a crescendo of speculative pain by the end of the book.

When I was judging the PEN awards, I discovered that Joy Williams, author of *The Visiting Privilege*, is a master of the art of literary devastation (described by writer Tracey Porter as the moment when "the protagonist is taken down by the very thing to which he has devoted himself"). Her uncannily observed and, perhaps, ultimately subversive short stories signify a direction in which I like to take my own work.

Fairie-ality by David Ellwand, an art book full of miniature fashions made out of insect wings and flower petals, had as much influence as any work of literature; it reached me so powerfully that it caused the hair to stand up on the back of my neck.

I discovered the following books, among others, from wonderfully eccentric bookseller-mentors, Jay and Jack of Dark Carnival Fantasy & Science Fiction Bookstore in Berkeley:

Bones of the Moon by Jonathon Carroll

Geek Love by Katherine Dunn

Moon Palace by Paul Auster

Sarah Canary by Karen Joy Fowler

Tapping the Source by Kem Nunn

The Circus of the Earth and the Air by Brooke Stevens

The Rule of the Bone by Russell Banks

The Tribes of Palos Verdes by Joy Nicholson

The Virgin Suicides by Jeffrey Eugenides

The White Bone and *We So Seldom Look on Love* by Barbara Goudy

Winterland by Elizabeth Hand

I can easily, magically lose myself in these ingenious voices and plot-rich stories, and they remind me why I love reading.

What are the books that mentored you at different phases of your life?

At the restaurant, Angel had handed me the ubiquitous LA actor headshot. He'd co-starred as the sexually confused youngest member of a romantic triangle in an indie movie and played drums in a band he'd formed with three of his five wry, black-haired brothers.

When I met Angel, I was living in a ridiculously affordable second-floor Spanish two-bedroom on Hayworth off Fairfax, near all the little Kosher markets and bakeries and pizza parlors and Canter's deli where the hipsters hung all night, sharing the place with my peppy roommate and her boyfriend. Angel and I heard their moans through the walls while we made love.

Angel and I had only been dating a few months when one of his brothers asked him to join a band in San Francisco. I didn't think I could live without him so we decided to move together. He went up first and found a Victorian gingerbread apartment building with a bay window, white floral stamped tin wainscoting on the walls, a marble fireplace, and newly finished wooden floors. Then he came to get me.

We'd stopped for gas on I-5, and when Angel was in the restroom, a man in sunglasses and his Doberman approached the truck. I've never felt so sure that someone wanted to do me harm. Angel came back just in time and the man walked away. Still wracked with shivers, I tried to explain but my boyfriend teased me about paranoia. A few hours later we were in our Victorian love nest, hanging pictures on the wall, picnicking on the floor, sleeping on the frameless futon mat after Angel had comforted me from the inside out. The killer on the road was long gone, but somehow it felt as if death shadowed me, stalked me from within.

To keep those feelings at bay I spent my days running to the gym and back, taking yoga classes, and unsuccessfully applying for jobs. The best two things I did were to get in touch with a few women I'd known from college and start a small writing circle in my apartment. There I began to write a second book about my new muse, Angel, and realized that I'd experienced a bit of beginner's luck the first time.

With no formal training, I'd pieced my debut book together from snippets of fairy tales, Greek myths, rock and punk lyrics, modernist poetry, and the Latin American magical realism I'd read as if I were eating guava pastries from the Tropicana Bakery on Sunset Boulevard in LA (which I missed now almost as much as I had while at Berkeley). The sequel, when delivered, had to be extensively rewritten with the help of my editor.

At night in San Francisco, I cooked organic, vegetarian meals for Angel and myself but he was almost never home. He worked as a waiter all day and took acting classes or played gigs at night. When he returned, late, my body thrilled to the feel of him slipping in next to me, sliding into me; it was what I lived for, those moments in bed, my lover's hair cool against my skin, his graceful body, constantly in motion.

Once I woke up laughing in my sleep. A belly laugh, orgasmic.

"What's so funny?" he asked.

"I had a dream."

"What was it? I had a dream, too. Mine was about a monkey."

"What?!"

"A wind-up monkey. Playing drums."

"In a red stocking hat?"

"With a pompom. How'd you know?"

"How did *you* know?'

I marveled at Angel's existence: How could this soul be in this body and have come into my arms at this point in space and time, I wondered. He was like a socket I needed to plug into, to feel alive.

I sickened with longing when he wasn't there, worried that he would fall in love with one of the many women he flirted with wherever he went, that this dream would end and I'd wake up alone, back in Los Angeles without muse or lover.

But soon after, I single-handedly made my fear a reality, said an emotional goodbye to Angel, and moved home to a courtyard bungalow apartment, painted turquoise blue, and situated just off Melrose. I resumed my retail job at Aphrodite's store, where I

{ My true muse has always been my alter ego. }

worked with a girl named Ping whose hair resembled a bird of paradise flower.

One day a couple came into the store. She looked like Belinda Carlisle from the Go-Go's and had a similar "punk Marilyn" style. When she left, Ping and I discovered a pair of pink vintage sunglasses with green lenses and she suggested I keep them. So I did. A few weeks later I was driving on the

405 and the boyfriend spotted me wearing the glasses. He came into the store and demanded them back. It was my one and only foray into a life of petty crime.

Angel returned a few months later and I begged him to move in with me but we both knew there was no room in the tiny studio. Still, we tried to resume our relationship.

Eventually my first book came out to positive, if sparse, reviews. At the launch party, Angel poured white wine into plastic cups and introduced himself as my "friend" to all the pretty young women he met.

That Halloween we dressed up as dead surfers in green face paint, seaweed strands, and Angel's wetsuits. We went to hear Smoke's new band Kooks play, and on the way home Angel and I talked about having babies.

"I'll make you vegan food and drive you to yoga every day," he said.

That same night we broke up, though I have no memory of what actually happened. "You should be with someone like Smoke," Angel said.

I went to my mother's house, got in the bathtub, and sobbed and shook for hours, as if I lay in a vat of ice water to cool a dangerously high fever.

I didn't date for the next three years.

My skin boiled with acne cysts brought on by stress and a facial gone wrong, and I was prescribed a powerful, toxic drug with pictures of deformed fetuses on each individual pill and warnings about bowel and liver disease and suicide on the label. Too depressed to leave the apartment, I cowered in loneliness watching *Juliet of the Spirits*, reading *Jane*

Eyre, and listening to Patti Smith while my upstairs neighbors slammed each other against the wooden floor.

There were no more men, or muses, to take my pain away.

ENCOURAGED BY MY editors and the prospect of another contract, I also spent my time in seclusion writing a book that dealt with the importance of letting go of those we have loved and lost.

I knew this was true but I hadn't learned the lesson yet.

When my skin healed, leaving scars around my mouth and on my chin, I called Angel, whose number had ingrained itself in my brain, though I had stricken it from my phone book.

"I want to be with you again," I told him, tears working their way from my throat to my eyes. We were at the park above PCH, where we had gone on our first date to watch the fireworks. That had been a warm night in early summer and this was a cold afternoon. The heart-shaped plot of ground around the statue of St. Mary sprouted yellow grass.

"There's something I have to tell you," he said.

I didn't want to hear. My heart was dirt and weeds.

"When we were living in San Francisco I slept with someone," he told me.

What he really meant was, "I can't do this again."

The full impact of my father's death, softened by my time with Angel and my cocoon-like years alone, came back with a vengeance. Maybe I'd find another muse, I thought, but never a lover. So I devoted myself to my writing more than ever.

A few months later, Smoke attended a reading for my latest book at a small café on Beverly Boulevard. He wore a leather motorcycle jacket with an angel painted on the back. As he watched me read I could see that something had changed.

I was witching him with my words.

A week later, Smoke and I helped our friend Drake move to Joshua Tree, where he opened a recording studio. The three of us hiked to a hidden waterfall oasis. We washed mushrooms down with milk in the moonlit monument. We barbecued corn on the grill, and I danced as Drake and Smoke played drums and sang. On the way back Smoke and I stopped at a roadside carnival and rode a Ferris wheel. When I got home I happened to browse through a ten-year-old dream journal and found an entry that read, "Smoke and I are riding a Ferris wheel together."

The next weekend we went back to the desert to see Drake and fell asleep by his hot tub, the embers of the fire pit still smoldering in the dark. Smoke and I woke and made love for the second time in ten years. In the morning a roadrunner dashed by, knocking a beer can onto our heads.

A month after that we were living together down the road from Drake in a pink adobe called Casa Rosa. (When I saw the name on the sign in front I immediately thought of Frida Kahlo's blue La Casa Azul in Mexico.) Rabbits scampered outside our window in the dawn light, and those trickster roadrunners dashed by. We wrote a screenplay together, made corn tortillas on the stovetop, and shared a joint and cherry vanilla frozen yogurt from the carton while watching horror movies from the creepy local video store at night.

One day we were outside Casa Rosa painting at easels when I felt something skitter around my foot. I bent down and picked up a small piece of paper covered in instructions on how to paint with oils and acrylics. It was a note my father had once written me—it had somehow followed me out to the desert and delivered itself into my hands at the perfect moment, as if he were truly watching over us, trying to inspire me from beyond the grave.

IN SPITE OF all the signs of magic, a sense of foreboding lingered. The street Smoke and I lived on was called Harmz Way.

One day, Smoke's ex-girlfriend and former band mate, Glinda, called. Her daughter, Eden, needed surgery related to the cancer she'd survived as a child. Smoke flew to Colorado to stay with Glinda and Eden at the Children's Hospital, then he came back for me and we drove to Colorado together to help however we could.

Iggy Pop's *American Caesar* was our constant soundtrack, and we stopped at national monuments, flinching at the sight of men in orange suits with deer carcasses in the back of their trucks. We stayed in motels with dripping faucets, hair in the drains, and, in one case, crime scene tape around the perimeter.

In Colorado, we subsisted on $5 tofu and white rice bowls from a tiny Japanese fast-food restaurant. Smoke sat at Eden's bedside for days, reading her poetry and singing to her. Her mother had posted pictures of her glamming, dancing teenager on the walls of the dark hospital room so that the doctors and nurses would see that there was more to this child than a mute, frozen, fragile body in a metal cast and Converse. I wandered the halls of that hospital, praying, and found wards full of children with shaved heads and a room of sterile metal tubs used to treat young burn victims.

When Eden had sufficiently recovered, Smoke and I flew to Chicago to see a play based on my book. At a cast party afterward, a tall, dark actor told me that everyone there was descended from a fairy race, that we had once been warriors and been driven underground and our ancestors had emerged to spawn us in the crazy world.

Soon after this surreal experience, Smoke and I moved back to Los Angeles. In some ways we were closer than ever, relieved at Eden's recovery, but our relationship also felt strained. One night, we drove through the hills of Laurel Canyon near where he'd gone to elementary school, hung out and gotten high with rock stars and film stars. The air was cool and fragrant, the atmosphere wooded. Deer and coyote watched us from the brush. There are parts of Los Angeles, just minutes away from highways and sky-scrapers, where you don't feel the city at all.

> When we write from our deepest longings, our stories have broader appeal.

We parked on Mulholland, looking down at the glister of lights below. I knew a few high school kids who'd died on that road in car wrecks.

"I wanted to ask you something," Smoke said, turning to me, his face barred with shadow. In those years since we'd first met, his hair had grown out to its original dark blond; his eyes hadn't been lined with black pencil in a decade.

I waited, watching our breath fog up the windows. My dog, Vincent Van Go-Go Boots, a springer spaniel with four white "boots," whom we'd found abandoned at a gas station near the Vincent Avenue exit on the way to Joshua Tree, put his head heavy and warm on my lap and sighed.

"I wanted to take you to the place I grew up," Smoke said. "So I could ask you to marry me."

I thought of the time a few months before when I'd flown to New York to meet him. He was staying with his actress friend Lovely and her cello-playing, model roommate. They were both glossy as pearls in vintage leopard coats and red lipstick. Once Smoke had said, "I'm glad I'm with you. I used to think I wanted to be with one of those really pretty girls. Like Winona Ryder or someone." Lovely looked a little like Winona Ryder, but prettier.

Smoke and I had exchanged silver rings before he'd left for New York. He had not been wearing his ring when he'd picked me up at the airport.

"Why'd you take it off?" I'd asked.

"No reason. It was just a little uncomfortable."

Neither of these things was so egregious, but the fact that they were what I thought of when he proposed to me told me that I wasn't ready to marry him. Not only because of my ever-present insecurities and fears, but also, perhaps, because of some premonitory instinct involving our futures and the children we were both destined to have with other people.

In the Jeep on Mulholland I was crying, and they weren't tears of joy.

"I guess that means no," Smoke said.

I SPENT THE next year turning the pieces I'd written about Smoke, Thorn, and Angel into a novel told in a series of short stories from the painter protagonist's first person point of view alternating with third person POVs of the other characters. Echo falls in love with different men, including a singer with haunting eyes, a poetic college student, and a troubled actor who is being slowly bled to death by his sister and her body-building boyfriend. It is only through her art that Echo ultimately gathers and assembles the fragments of her identity.

I wrote not because anyone was paying me to do so or telling me they liked my words.

I kept writing because it felt like the only way I could survive.

OBSESSIONS

When we write from our deepest longings, our stories have broader appeal.

Much of my writing comes out of a sense of freedom to explore the things that interest or obsess me. This was another gift from my parents, who encouraged my play as a child—my mother by endlessly feeding my bisque doll and Victorian dollhouse fetish and my father by letting me collaborate with him on drawings of frolicking fauns and nymphs.

My favorite pastime was to walk in circles around the eucalyptus-pod-paved backyard, twirling a curl of hair on one finger, sucking my lower lip, and making up stories. If I made a "mistake," I forced myself to start over from the beginning. It might have looked like an obsessive-compulsive disorder, but for me this was the "play" that would lead to a career as a writer.

In order to get in touch with your obsessions, try making a list of anything that fascinates you. Be as specific and detailed as possible. Instead of "trees" or "flowers," identify the kind of flora that delights you. Instead of "food," try, "the freshly pickled kimchee I just ate out of the jar from the Korean stand, among bushels of roses and dahlias, buckets of oysters, clouds of incense and barbecue smoke, and the sounds of a clown twisting balloons into animals at the downtown Culver City farmer's market."

Don't worry if anyone else finds the subject interesting—what is important is how much you are intrigued and how you can convey that through specificity and passion!

When writing my first book, I included the things that intrigued me at the time, not thinking that anyone else outside of my immediate circle of friends would care much about them, especially in combination:

Punk rock

Fairy tales

Wiener dogs

Bleached hair

Mohawks

Classic cars

Vintage prom dresses

Pink and black Doc Marten creepers

Surfers

Pacific Ocean

Santa Ana winds

Pink smog sunsets

The moon

The canyons

Jacaranda trees

Oleander bushes

Hollywood in Miniature

Strawberry marshmallow sundaes from Schwab's Pharmacy

The cuckoo clocks on the walls of Tick Tock Tea Room

Vinyl shoppers from the Farmer's Market

The stars on Hollywood Boulevard

Picnics at the Hollywood sign

This first short novel became my most popular and widely published book. I can only explain its success by the idea that it was not the items on the list that still appeal to people in, say, Japan and Norway, but the specificity and impassioned energy behind my depictions.

Of course, our obsessions and delights change as time passes. If you were to ask me today about my obsessions, I might say:

My children's faces

My slinkster dog Elphi's teddy bear chest and belly, fox fur, monkey tail, and alligator jaw

Yoga flow to Sinead O'Connor, PJ Harvey, Hole, Nir-
    vana, Patti Smith

Vegan Caesar salad wraps from Café Gratitude

Green tea bobas with almond milk

Pink peonies in large cylindrical glass vases

Pink purses with silver hardware

Fairy lights

Frida Kahlo paintings

David Bowie

Talking about books with My Secret Man

Remember, it is not the subjective things themselves that
matter as much as our desire for them and what they represent: in my case **the universal yearning for sustenance,
love, beauty, and healing.**

YOU MIGHT SEE your afflatus, your muse, embodied as an
artist, designer, writer, singer, dancer, actor, or historical
figure—Frida Kahlo, Virginia Woolf, Coco Chanel, Yves St.
Laurent, Alexander McQueen, Jimi Hendrix, Kurt Cobain,
Isadora Duncan, Vaslav Nijinski, Audrey Hepburn, James
Dean, Marilyn, Martin Luther King—but anyone you admire
will do.

The more I write, the more I realize that my muse wasn't
Cat Stevens or any of my boyfriends. My true muse has always been the protagonist of my first book, a bleach-blond
fairy named from the license plate I'd seen on a Bazooka-
bubblegum-pink Pinto on the 405 when I was sixteen, that

girl in rhinestone-studded rose-colored Harlequin sunglasses and a pair of roller skates, that girl who would grow up, find true love and family, find herself. In other words, my muse was my alter ego, a distinct, if internalized, part of me.

After hearing the news of David Bowie's death in January 2016, I couldn't stop seeing his face in my mind. Or should I say faces—he had so many identities. But there was only one clear, elegant yet playful message from Mr. Bowie, and at least three of my friends heard it, too: *You must write*. I'd been stuck for almost a year, trying to churn out bad romance ebooks to make a living, but with Bowie's death came a new burst of creativity.

It began as an outpouring of random scenes from my life and became a series of essays about how Bowie had touched me with his work and finally evolved into this memoir/creative manifesto. Once again, the muse started out as someone outside of me but became internalized over time.

The writer, blogger, and lifestyle icon Gala Darling, with her floral tattoos, over-the-knee boots, Cleopatra hair and eyeliner, and hot pink lipstick and matching faux fur jackets, worships Diana Vreeland the way I love the current editor of French *Vogue* Emmanuelle Alt, effortlessly chic in a uniform of skinny jeans, rocker T-shirts, and motorcycle or military jackets or leopard coats, impossibly strutting around Paris on stilettos with her assistant and young daughter in tow.

My agent, Erin Hosier, told me, "I think my muse is fear." I can certainly relate, as you will see by reading the rest of this book.

Your muse could be a loved one, a parent, a spouse, or a child. Scott Blackwood, author of the PEN-award-winning *See How Small* cites as his muse his daughter Ellie, who was born when he was twenty-five years old and searching for his voice:

> What I discovered was, with a new baby and so many new demands, . . . I'd have to cut away the willfully naïve younger self to get anything written that was worth something. The willfully naïve younger self didn't want that, of course. But this younger self was a ruse, just an invented means to not commit to writing, to not take real risks, and to always have a ready reason why. So my daughter and all the changes she brought on (a female way of seeing in the world) led me to be a better writer—so much so that I wouldn't have written anything good without her because I wouldn't have known what to leave out or when to let things speak for themselves (selectivity and patience).

My muse has also been a place. Los Angeles, my alluring, toxic city. Virulent oleander bushes and belladonna lilies. Hot, violent Santa Ana winds of mica and sand. Canyons bleeding wildflowers and road kill. Acacia and jacaranda trees dying in the drought. Sunsets that burn and blister with smog. Peaceful-looking suburban homes, with empty swimming pools in the backyards, where drug use and child abuse rampaged through the 1970s.

My Los Angeles is also Joan Didion's endless, vacuous freeways "peopled" by cars like the 1965 aquamarine VW

Notchback that was stolen from my driveway—instant karma for those sunglasses I'd appropriated—and then reappeared in the Gladstone's parking lot along PCH where I'd gone to interview Perry Farrell and his band Porno for Pyros for *Spin*, and while I still had the key on my key ring; my 1981 black Mercedes convertible two-seater that had to be traded in for a Honda when I gave birth to my first child; or my black Jeep Cherokee, AKA Cherry, who should have been named after another sourer yellow fruit.

But ultimately the muse isn't really any of these people, places, or things. The muse, daughter of the sky and memory, is deep, deep inside, waiting to be called upon, more reliable than any idol, any lover.

Try to imagine your internal muse as a person. What does she look like? What does he have to say? Ask for help. If you pay attention, you will see, and if you listen you will hear.

CHILDHOOD WOUNDS

Wants and **needs**, as well as **gifts** and **flaws**, can come from a deep wound inflicted upon the protagonist as a child. The reader may not read about this childhood wound in a scene, and yet it influences the character throughout the story.

How does a writer know what wound to give a main character? Consider your own. Even if a story is not autobiographical, the wound that motivates the writer often appears on the page. It may be the single biggest reason for the drive to write a book at all.

Here are some examples **of childhood wounds** that influence the characters in our sample novels:

> In *To Kill a Mockingbird*, Scout, motherless at an early age, must find her way into adulthood without a woman as a role model.

> In *The Great Gatsby*, Gatsby lost Daisy and is desperate to reclaim her.

> In *Jane Eyre*, Jane was orphaned and endured the cruelty imposed upon her by her aunt and cousins. Her suffering conjures her sense of urgency to find a home of her own.

> In *Wuthering Heights*, Heathcliff was abandoned by his own family and never fully embraced by his adoptive one. His story is driven by his desire for true acceptance.

> In *Lolita*, a young Humbert was in love with a girl named Annabel Leigh. She died, driving Humbert to find a replacement in Lolita.

Without their wounds, these characters might be less enthralling, less able to stand the test of time. The same can be said of us as humans.

THE 12 QUESTIONS: WANTS AND NEEDS
Question #3 What does your character want?
Question #4: What does your character need?

Wants

The want of a character is something practical and concrete to which we, as humans, can all relate in some way.

In *To Kill a Mockingbird*, Scout wants to understand adulthood.

In *The Great Gatsby*, Gatsby wants Daisy.

In *Jane Eyre*, Jane wants to leave an unhappy home.

In *Wuthering Heights*, Heathcliff wants Catherine.

In *Lolita*, Humbert wants Dolores Haze, whom he nicknames Lolita.

In *Play It As It Lays*, Maria wants to drive on freeways to escape her life.

Each of these is symbolic of deeper human desires for happiness and connection, so that even if we abhor Humbert's hebephilia, for example, we can at least understand his desperation. When we understand Heathcliff's desire for Catherine, we are able to identify with him in spite of his cruelty later on. By giving the character a clear want from the beginning of the book, the writer will engage the reader in a number of ways.

A strong want will help the reader identify with and care about the character because he or she has desires, just as the reader does.

The want, if pursued, will make the character active. If the goal is understandable and not met, and the character is forced to work harder to meet it, the reader will admire the character's efforts and root for him or her. Remember, an active character is almost always a sympathetic, or at least relatable, character.

A goal that isn't met provides a strong story problem for a book. One of the biggest mistakes writers make is not having a clear story problem from the beginning (or sometimes at all). This, along with an engaging voice and sympathetic character, are the things readers (as well as agents and editors, if you're interested in finding them) look for on the very first page. However, story problems and sympathetic characters can be developed over the course of a rough draft.

A strong want engages the reader by raising the stakes. Wants should change and escalate over the course of the book as a means to further test the protagonist when the wants are not met, or met and then taken away. We see this in *Jane Eyre*: Jane achieves her want when she escapes Gateshead, the home of her cruel aunt and cousins. She then lives in an orphanage, where she develops a want for a home where she is accepted, which prompts her to become a governess at Thornfield Hall.

The more the writer shows how much the character covets the goal, the more the reader will begin to care about the outcome of the story and continue turning pages until the end.

Needs

A want is something conscious, concrete, and potentially obtainable, like the love of a specific person, or something material, even "superficial." The character is often aware of his or her want.

A need, however, is more secretive. **A need is deep-seated, psychological, and necessary for a character to grow**, though he or she may not be aware of it until the end of the book—if then. In a tragedy, for example, a character's demise is often caused by his own inability to determine what he needs. For instance, in *Wuthering Heights*, Heathcliff needs to overcome his cruelty in order to be loved. The fact that he doesn't— because he can't see his need the way the reader, and Catherine, can—is what makes *Wuthering Heights* a tragedy. The message it offers—that prejudice and unfairness breed cruelty and pain—is clearly demonstrated through the tortured, unaware soul of Heathcliff and his unmet need.

THE NEED OFFERS a path to resolution in the character's **arc**. Here are more examples:

> In *To Kill a Mockingbird*, Scout needs to develop compassion to tolerate the inequities in the world.
>
> In *The Great Gatsby*, Gatsby needs to let go of the past.
>
> In *Jane Eyre*, Jane needs to balance her passion and reason.
>
> In *Lolita*, Humbert needs to overcome his inappropriate sexual interest.
>
> In *Play It As It Lays*, Maria needs to keep "playing" for something meaningful (her daughter, Kate), to care and to love, not to give up or fall into the abyss.

The want is the initial obstacle that the character faces, while the need is the deeper story problem: Will Scout mature? Will Jane learn to follow both her heart *and* her mind? Will Heathcliff transcend the cruelty of his childhood and the disappointments and pain of his youth? Will Humbert abandon his perversely lustful ways? Will Maria give up and fall into the abyss or keep "playing" for her daughter, Kate?

Understanding a character's wants and needs puts a writer on the path to understanding her characters and navigating them through their experiences. At the same time, the writer learns of her own wants and needs, and finds her way toward fulfilling them.

3

BLOOD ROSES
—— Channel Pain into Art

A MONTH BEFORE I LEFT FOR COLLEGE AT BERKELEY, MY parents sat me down in the living room, their faces grave. "We have to tell you something."

They often spoke as if they were one person, and had taken to signing their names on my birthday cards, "Love MomPa." (Clearly boundaries weren't our family's strong suit.)

It was summer and the air lingered like a muse's breath on my skin, but I still clung to my dog Teddy for warmth. He sighed heavily with animal intuition and his heart thudded against my hand. Irises filled a blue and white Delft vase, their silky petals ridged with veins like those showing beneath the surface of my own thin wrist skin.

"I have cancer," my father said.

The prelude to my greatest childhood fear, the thing I'd worried about for as long as I could remember. It was almost as if I could feel the cells metastasizing in my own body. *I don't want to hear this.*

When I was a child and needed a hospital procedure that required a catheter, my mother stayed by my side, keeping me close, while the doctor inserted the tube into my bladder.

My father once knelt down on the floor and gathered me up in his arms when I'd hidden under a needlepoint bench, crying to the point of hysteria because a boy I liked had rejected me with violent words.

Neither of my parents could comfort me now.

I got up and went out through the heavy front door that my father had painted a pale shade of robin's egg. The oleander bushes radiant with heat. A murder of crows scattering into the sky as I started to run.

Down my street, sobbing. Boys in a car drove by, honked at my ass. They pulled up and saw my face. Puffy and red, streaked with black tears.

"Ugly!" they screamed and roared away.

The two things inexorably linked themselves in my mind:

The ones you love sicken and die; you are ugly, unlovable, leavable.

And this: *You are going to have to leave.*

THE WAY I tried to maintain some fragile and warped sense of self-worth during this time was through my academic success, my relationship with my boyfriend Thorn, and, later, an unhealthy obsession with limiting my caloric intake.

But, once again, only one thing really helped me survive: my writing.

I did not write directly about my father's illness or even my loneliness. After recovering, with my father's help, from the lukewarm reception of my first submission in the afore-mentioned writing workshop, I tried to reshape my experiences, creating short stories based on Greek myths and a book structured in the form of a tarot reading that tells of a damaged young woman's relationship with the mysterious man who comes through her window at night.

Although fathers die in many of the tales I told myself, these stories allowed me to escape into worlds of magic (either literal or the enchantment of figurative language) away from the reality of my life and the confines of a body I did not want to inhabit.

According to the American Psychological Association, expressive writing, prevalent in psychotherapy since the days of Carl Jung, has proven helpful as a healing tool. There is even recent evidence that such writing can reduce stress and boost the function of the immune system. However, Susan Lutgendorf, PhD, of the University of Iowa, conducted an intensive study on journaling that showed the key to success was not only the writing itself, which could even exacerbate negative feelings, but the ability to relive the emotions in a visceral way and find meaning in the traumatic event described.

For me, that meaning came through shaping my pain into art.

It takes distance to see pain properly. We all have it as fuel but tossing it into a story often backfires. Sometimes I reach an empathetic wall with the character and I have to wait until I can find a way into their sense of loss.

In *See How Small*, I was writing about a woman who'd lost her two teenage daughters, and I kept hitting the wall— I could not find a route to what this might be like to lose your whole world. Everything fell short. But then one day, my six-year-old daughter went missing from school and, in those 60 minutes—in a cab heading home, frantically calling neighbors, talking to the police, knowing suddenly that everything I'd taken for granted as solid ground was really an unstable fault line.

I eventually found my daughter. She was fine; she'd walked to a friend's house. But what life might be like without her spooled out in my head. Those moments, with some distance, allowed me to try again, to find the minor key of loss.

—SCOTT BLACKWOOD, author of *See How Small*, winner of the PEN USA Award for Fiction

MY FATHER LIVED for five more years after his diagnosis, mostly because of my mother's love and care, and, I think, his own determination not to abandon her. But one night, very late, in my bed in the house in the Berkeley hills, I got the call I'd been bracing for, clenching my jaw each night in my sleep, so hard that I'd already ground out one tooth and needed a root canal.

"It's Daddy," my mother said, her voice like paper crumpling. "Come home now."

By the time I flew to Burbank airport and arrived at the hospital, he was in a coma.

After he was taken off life support, my mom and I left the fluorescent, sterile room where his body lay like the flower in the painting he'd completed just days before—a fragile blood-black rose buffeted by white winds. Even his last image conveyed the same message: *Pain can become art.*

Dazed, my mom and I drove to Fryman Canyon. A dirt path led up among eucalyptus trees to a smog-scrimmed view of the city. On our way back down we passed a field that we had walked by many times before. A white horse we had never seen there ran toward us across the grass and pressed the tender velvet of its nose (soft as the wild red roses that grew) against the metal fence, staring at us with a kind of knowing, its eyes dark, bright worlds. We wept with grief, but also awe. It seemed clear that my father's spirit was communing with us.

My mom and brother and my friend Dirk drove me up to Berkeley the next week for my graduation. There was a letter in my mailbox from my father; he'd mailed it the day he died. The letter, in his spidery, elegant hand, said how much he loved me, how much he was looking forward to spending time with me—talking about art and poetry, going to museums and movies, eating Japanese food, reading my stories.

He reminded me, "Let go of guilt, let happiness be your closest friend." Maybe I never got to say goodbye, but my father did.

As my family and friends and I walked along Telegraph after the ceremony, I saw something on the sidewalk and reached to pick it up without thinking or even realizing what it was—a small green plastic cowboy astride a white plastic horse.

"It's Daddy," my mother said again, this time meaning something very different, as I put it into the pocket of the white linen suit I'd bought with money I'd won from my short stories and poetry.

My father had never lived to see me published but he'd known about those awards, proof of what he had shouted at me that night in my dorm room.

White horses haunted my mother for years afterward—in photographs, books, and films. She believed they were messengers from my father. This notion helped her cope with the loss but also somehow kept her from being fully present. Instead of taking dance classes, writing poetry, and creating the collages she promised herself she'd make, she filled journals with her dreams about my father and recorded tapes of her voice keening for him to somehow return to her.

Without her beloved, my mother dwelled in some kind of netherworld of psychopomps, ghosts, and angels.

I MIGHT HAVE lived in the underworld, too, but instead I wrote about a girl with an artist father and a Botticelli-Venus-like mother who falls in love with Death when her husband passes away. Because it felt too painful to write directly about what had happened, I used magic to distance the story from reality and to heighten the dramatic impact. The mother is a kind of "kitchen witch," the father literally becomes a white horse, death is an actual character, and the girl encounters angels and vampires.

"I want to go with him," my mother said one night as we lay on her rose velvet living room couches, head to head, trying to sleep.

"No, you're not going anywhere, I won't let you," I told her. I could feel my soul pulling at hers, tugging her back. The process took its toll on my body: Over the next few years I developed chronic fatigue, nodules on my thyroid, the cystic acne that would be treated by those pills with the alien babies on each one.

My mother didn't want to be alone and I was afraid to leave her. I took her out to see foreign and indie films, to restorative yoga classes, and on hikes, bought her organic carrot juice and macrobiotic meals. In some ways I became her substitute for my father, though she also tried to find him in a series of men for whom she recreated her role as muse. The sweet-faced, forever boyish photographer who took nude pictures of her. The embittered holocaust survivor who wrote her stories. The relative of my father's who sent her torrid love letters that I found many years later. And the married artist with the same cancer my father had had, who painted her as a seductive temptress, complete with apple and serpent, and told her, "You are the reason I'm still alive," but then died, leaving her broken once again.

MY MOTHER LEARNED she had cancer a few months after her lover's death, and almost thirty years after my father's.

The night she called to tell me she'd found blood in her urine and had gone to a doctor, I'd been on FU Cupid, corresponding with a black-haired, pale-eyed man in his forties who shared the name of the love interest in the book I was currently writing.

My children, then seven and nine, were marching through the living room, tooting on plastic horns, beating drums, and holding up signs that said "We love Mom" when my mother called.

When I hung up the phone, I closed the dating site from my screen and took my children in my arms. Their hair smelled like chamomile soap from their baths. I'd never clung so tightly to them.

After they'd gone to sleep I called the man from the dating website and told him that I'd just learned my mother was sick.

"I'd like to help you," he said.

I did not question the oddness of this. In my stricken state I thought, *He has come to save me! He is magic!*

On our first date, he picked me up in an old black hearse that smelled pleasantly of clove cigarette smoke. He wore a top hat and vintage tuxedo shirt with his black jeans and Doc Martens. As macabre as it was, the pageantry of the whole thing intrigued me. My children sat in the window watching us drive off before my mother called them away from the window. The man and I went to dinner and then walked through downtown Culver City.

The trees were strung with Christmas lights and the air was cooling toward autumn, lightly fragrant with smoke. An eerie bronze man read a newspaper on a bench. A lion sculpture danced in a fountain. In the window of the Culver Hotel dolls cavorted, dressed as characters from *The Wizard of Oz*.

My date picked a white calla lily that grew in front of a white mansion, now Sony offices, that had been used for Tara in *Gone with the Wind*, and handed it to me. His face was gaunt with a high brow, pale as the lily in the street lamp light. I was trying hard not to think about the illness crawling through my mother's organs.

A short time later, the man drove me to a motel near the hospital so I could be there in the morning when my mom had her surgery. A grinning metal head—horned and bearded and demonic—hung on the door of the motel room down the hall, and I stopped to stare at it.

"What is that?"

We looked at each other.

Neither of us spoke the word: *Devil*.

My mother survived her surgery and came home frail and hunched and in pain, part of her body missing, but she was alive. About the man, she said, "He's the only one you've been with who is worthy of you."

Her illness had obviously addled both my mother and me.

One night, late, the man and I went to his home to watch *The Lord of the Rings*.

"It's actually my ex-stepfather's," he said when we arrived at the ranch house at the end of a dirt road.

We went upstairs to a bedroom decorated in Victorian furniture. On the dresser sat a picture of the man and an older woman with their arms around each other.

"This is my mother's room," he said.

He slept next door in what amounted to his mother's closet. Her dresses hung in plastic bags along the walls, leaving almost no room even for a small bed.

> You may be recovering from a broken heart or grieving for the fraught state of this fragile world. The ways of pain are infinite, and it's easy to be consumed.

I ignored all this; someone was caring for me while my mother was dying. I did not realize how much my reaction to my mother's illness mirrored her response to my father's death. Now I was the one seeking the underworld for myself. If my mother was going to go there, I would follow her loyally into the shadows.

THREE MONTHS AFTER my mom's surgery I went to my ophthalmologist because one of my eyes appeared red and irritated. I tried to read the chart with it, but it didn't go well, and soon the tech stopped me.

"I'll get the doctor."

I covered my right eye and looked through my left at the chart in front of me. A black shadow obscured half of my vision. I'd been so consumed with my mom that I hadn't noticed my retina had been spontaneously tearing in half.

I had an emergency vitrectomy a few days later; a surgeon placed a buckle around my retina, saving the remaining vision. My mom was too sick and my brother too busy caring for her to help much, so the man drove me in his hearse to and from the surgery appointment and put me to bed, where I had to lie for a week without getting up, my head hanging off the edge in order to help fluid drain from the eye. He stood at my bedside wringing his hands as I begged for Xanax and mumbled from a haze of anesthesia and Oxycodone that I wanted to die. I didn't blame him for his immobilizing distress; it was all too much.

Most of my friends couldn't bear to see me this way and rarely visited. The nurse my mother and brother hired scolded me for not catching the signs earlier (though I'd never noticed any) and told me all about her friend who went suddenly and completely blind in both eyes from the same disease. Only Esmeralda, who'd helped me raise my children since they were babies, was able to comfort me.

She brought me fresh young coconuts to sip from, gave me sponge baths, crooned to me in her soft voice, "*Bonita, bonita,*" as her black horse's mane tickled my cheeks. She comforted my frightened children who were staying with their dad at the time, gently detangling the elflocks that had ravaged my daughter's curls while she was away from me.

When I no longer had to lie with my head hanging off the bed, my brother brought my mom over. She hobbled in and sat at my bedside reading the galleys of my next book aloud to me, since I still hadn't adjusted to the eye patch I had to wear, and making my corrections on the manuscript.

I remember this as a time of great comfort and connection between us.

The book is about a young woman who is consumed with an animal rage (the result of a family curse) and tries to kill her mother when she returns from a hunting spree. Later, the mother shoots her daughter, mistaking her for a wolf, and the girl loses her hand. It is replaced with a hand of silver. Inspired by the fairy tale "The Handless Maiden"; by my feelings about animal rights, racism, and homophobia; and by a certain shrill female politician with a penchant for hunting, the story provided me with catharsis during a difficult time.

My mom, who cringed at violence, helped me with this book in spite of its disturbing content. But in the remaining months she began to retreat deeper into herself, unwilling to come live with me as I'd offered, spending her days meditating and praying to the Tibetan goddess Tara. I brought her vegan dinners, and we sat and watched foreign films a few nights a week.

When I wasn't with her, I cared for my children, or, on weekends when they were with their father, I saw the man. He took me to a late-night steak restaurant where we sat in a red vinyl booth and I watched him eat a rare steak and drink a dirty martini. Later, he drove me back with him, to sleep in his mother's closet.

In the morning, she entered without knocking. (It was her closet after all.) We were lying in bed. The day was hot, the air in the closet close and humid. The plastic bags over the dresses threatened to suffocate us. My boyfriend's mother stood there in her satin slip, her iron-gray Viking braids falling over her large, loose breasts.

"A girl just came by to see you," she told him. "I said you were busy." She frowned at me. "That's terrible about your eye. A friend of mine got flashes and floaters and ignored them. She should have known better. She lost the whole eye, actually. Such a shame." She turned to go. "I'm surprised you didn't have any warning signs," she said.

HIKING THE ARC

Arcs are best served by an active character.

When I write my own story, I often end up with pages of passive exposition rather than active scenes, even though I know that this is almost always ineffectual.

The excess exposition in memoir comes from being engulfed in a tidal wave of vague memories that haven't solidified into scenes yet, and, in turn, the result is a passive "character"—me!—who feels and thinks but doesn't "do" much.

Then, as I rework my writing, I think about Cheryl Strayed's *Wild*. In *Wild*, the author actively *does* something challenging and dangerous. She flashes to *memories* of her dead mother and dying marriage, but the through-line is the Pacific Crest Trail hike itself. Her actions offer a structure to steer the narrative; her memories provide the emotional impetus to keep her moving forward.

I haven't hiked much, but I've loved, lost, married, divorced, raised children, battled illness, and taught thousands of students. This is my Pacific Trail.

What's yours?

ONE SWELTERING DAY in September, my mother called me on the phone. "Can you come over?" she whispered. "My hands are so cold. I need you to warm them. I don't like the people here."

I drove to the Spanish-style one-bedroom apartment she'd recently rented so she could be closer to my brother and me. It was still full of boxes of books, papers, journals, paintings, and art supplies she hadn't unpacked. While she dozed I sat at her bedside and held her hands. Her body had shrunken even more. The hospice people were talking in the other room.

"Yeah, seventy-eight-year-old female, she has colon cancer. Spread to the bladder. I think it's in the bones now, too."

"What do you want for lunch?"

I marched into the kitchen. "Can you please shut up? She's trying to rest. We can hear you. You can leave now."

I went back to my mother. I should have been comforting her but: "Everything is going to be okay," she told me. She gestured to her disease-riddled body. "Except this." She chuckled to herself. "Is Zack coming?" she asked.

My heart felt stuffed with pain, as those boxes full of things littering her living room. It was time. I called my brother. "Come now."

While I waited, my mother murmured in her sleep and I sat on the floor and finished the epilogue to the novel that I'd started a year and a half earlier. It's about a young UC Berkeley college student who must search for her missing friend, a search that will take the protagonist into a dark, erotic world and, eventually, to the edge of madness. Ironically, I'd begun to write the book six months before I knew my mom was sick, and Ariel's mother is diagnosed with cancer in the first chapter. I finished this disturbingly prophetic novel an hour before my mother passed away.

AT SUNDOWN ON Yom Kippur 2010, Zack and I sat on either side of our mom in the darkened room. She woke and seemed suddenly changed, her face illuminated from within, her green eyes round and shining as she looked from one to the other of us, then reached out like a prima ballerina at curtain call and took our hands. We wept, lowering our heads to hide our tears, to no avail, and distress contorted her face; she looked like a stricken child.

"It's okay," I told her. "We're just sad because we love you so much. But you can go if you need to. We'll be okay. We'll take care of each other. Like you said, everything will be okay."

My mother smiled.

That smile like Marilyn Monroe's that had charmed so many people in her lifetime. That smile of golden beads that had led me to write love poems to the goddess. She continued to smile, looking into my brother's eyes and then mine and back again. She looked to the foot of the bed and raised her palm in a gesture that seemed to mean, *Not now. Not yet.*

I wondered: *Who stood there?*

She looked back into our eyes, my brother's and then mine. Then she seemed to shudder with the first grip of death's claw, and my brother administered the drop of morphine into her mouth as he'd been instructed; she took it like a baby bird. Smiling, still, beaming avatar light, she looked to the foot of the bed. She nodded to whatever phantom awaited her there. I imagined it was my father. Finally she had found him again. She closed her eyes and left us.

Would I spend the rest of my life waiting to rejoin my parents as my mother had spent hers awaiting this reunion with her husband?

My brother left the room, and I changed my mother's clothes, put her in clean pink cotton pajamas. Her limbs were rigid as I'd heard they would be, though I was in no way prepared for how a corpse (*my mother is a corpse?*) felt. Still, I managed to gently wrestle her clothing onto her and kiss her face. The effulgent light had gone from it.

By her bedside were the two necklaces she always wore—a silver chain with a Tara pendant, and a golden chain with a mother-of-pearl bead from which dangled three rings—a turquoise one from my childhood, my father's baby ring, and her wedding band. I put the two chains around my neck and wrapped my mother in a sheet.

Zack and I waited while the paramedics came. I drove home alone in that crepuscular hour, nauseated, and buried into bed like an animal. I wanted to turn myself inside out, to escape the confines of my body in any way possible.

But in the morning, when I put her necklaces around my own neck, I could hear my mother's voice as if her spirit had slipped inside the locket. "I love you, darling," she said. "Keep writing. Keep loving. Everything will be all right."

Would it? The vespertine man came over to my house with the darkness. He crouched on my bed, his arms around his legs, he rocked his body back and forth. If I closed my good eye I could only see half of him; the shadow cut off the top of his head.

"What's wrong?" I said.

He peeked up from his knees. He pointed his finger. "There's something there," he said. "There. Behind you. It's your mother."

I swallowed both an Ambien and an Oxycodone left over from my eye surgery and turned off the light.

"Can I come in?" he asked later, hovering above me in the dark. It was hard to speak, for obvious reasons. I didn't say no.

In the morning I told him to leave. I attended a yoga workshop on opening the heart and cried for the entire two hours. My brother drove me home and stayed with me as night fell. I found the encroaching darkness terrifying to face alone since my loss of vision.

He wanted to understand why I'd been so utterly felled by that shadow in my eye.

"It's like a circuit was broken," I said. I held up an electrical cord. "It's like this has been pulled and I can't connect it anymore. I need you to connect it, and I'll put my hand on your arm while you do it. I'm sorry. Does that make sense at all?"

My brother nodded and took the cord from my hand. "I'll do that for you," he said.

The man and I broke up the next day. Then I began to write the story of what had happened. In my version, a pale, dark-haired man takes a woman to a fairy world from which she cannot return, until her children call her back. I published it in a collection a few years later.

This man might have been mentally unstable during our time together, but obviously, like Ariel from my novel, so was I. In fact, I think I'd lost my mind at the time, so consumed with grief that it quite possibly, literally, blinded me.

But now everything was "all right," as my mother had predicted. I had continued to write my way through, just as I did in the gloaming of that autumnal equinox, sitting on my mother's bedroom floor, while the chatty hospice women packed up and went home to their families and my mother slept, awaiting my brother's arrival so she could let go and leave us.

It was clear to me that my mother had died in some essential way after my father did. Maybe she would have actually died at that time if I had not needed her so much to stay, just as my children needed me.

Because of my love for them and what my parents had taught me about the healing powers of art, I knew I would survive.

EVERYONE EXPERIENCES PAIN. You may have lost a loved one or suffered through a serious illness. You may be recovering from a broken heart or grieving for the fraught state of this fragile world. The ways of pain are infinite and it's easy to be consumed. My mother, ultimately, was. She never wrote the poetry or made the collages she'd intended to create, though I did discover her best poem, about Colon Cancer coming to call ("he liked what he heard/he liked what he saw") in a journal by her bedside; she had written it just before she died.

Frida Kahlo had polio as a child, survived a horrific accident at eighteen that shattered her body and pierced her pelvis with an iron hand rail, and suffered through a number of resulting miscarriages. To add insult to injury, her husband, the muralist Diego Rivera, had an affair with her younger sister.

But Frida produced hundreds of works of art, including the fifty-five famed self-portraits—crow-wing brows and head flowering with images of her beloved betrayer—that elevate unbearable grief to shocking beauty.

> Some artists survive their pain, some do not. But all channel it into art.

Her painting *Self-Portrait with Thorn Necklace and Hummingbird*, for which this book is named, expresses pain and martyrdom through the image of the thorns, and hope through the hummingbird, which was often worn, in Mexico, as a charm to bring luck in love.

Sylvia Plath, Anne Sexton, and Virginia Woolf took their own lives but wrote some of the most powerful poetry and prose of the twentieth century. Vincent van Gogh withstood poverty, bouts of anxiety, and mental illness, eventually shooting himself at the age of thirty-seven, but left behind thousands of drawings and oil paintings swirling with the vivid undercurrent of spirit and transcending the great tragedy of his existence. The writers Hans Christian Andersen, Charles Baudelaire, John Keats, Edgar Allan Poe,

T. S. Eliot, Ezra Pound, William Faulkner, Ernest Hemingway, and Raymond Chandler, and the artists Edgar Degas, Edvard Munch, Paul Gauguin, and Mark Rothko struggled with depression. Some artists survive their pain, some do not. But all channel it.

TAKE YOUR TIME and channel your grief and loss into art. In this way our pain, and our lives, and perhaps the world itself, can be profoundly transformed.

THE 12 QUESTIONS: ARC
Question #5: What is your character's arc?

TO DEFINE YOUR character's **arc**, think of the state of mind that the character is in at the beginning of the story and the state of mind she is in at the end. Unless the book is a tragedy, the character's arc usually goes from a negative to a positive state. Between the two states are a series of scenes of escalating conflict, all pushing the main character toward a resolution.

That journey, from start to finish, is the arc.

The arc often begins with a **want**. This want pushes the character into the world to seek some kind of change. For example, Jane Eyre leaves the Lowood orphanage to work as a governess at Thornfield, driven by her want to become more independent.

The character's need is usually the same as the final state of the character at the end of his arc.

In other words, the character arc goes from "**flaw**" to "**need**." (Jane moves from alternating impetuousness and self-denial to a balance of passion and reason.) This process can be torturous, pushing the character to her very limits and making her confront obstacles that seem insurmountable. I used to think that stacking up obstacles against a character was enough to make him sympathetic but have since learned that how he grows in the face of these obstacles is what counts.

In *To Kill a Mockingbird*, Scout's arc is a classic coming-of-age arc. She changes from a somewhat prejudiced child (flaw) to a wiser, compassionate young woman (need). Her strength—an innate stubbornness—serves her well here, as she encounters the challenges of school and defends her family to others. But her stubbornness also gets in the way of her growth, and creates the needed tension in the book. Ultimately, however, her love and loyalty to her family, as well as Atticus's teachings and the circumstances she faces, help her to fully open her heart to others and see the truth about Boo Radley. Meeting her need, to grow up and become more open minded, is the same as the culmination of her arc.

The Great Gatsby has a tragic ending, as Jay Gatsby never traverses an arc from his flaw (obsessive ambition) to his need (to give up the past and live in the present). However, Nick, the narrator, does: He learns a lesson from Gatsby's tragic end and gives up the superficial world of the East to return home to the West. Nick's need—to make sense of society and find a place for himself—is met at the end of his arc.

The character's **gift** also helps along the arc. Although Jane's excessive passion and reason get her into trouble, they are also the qualities that, when balanced, lead her back not only to Rochester but to herself. Often a **flaw** reveals itself at the beginning of the arc, too. Overcoming the flaw can be the test the character must pass to reach the culmination of the arc.

Readers who feel a human connection with a character, through a set of clearly defined wants, needs, gifts, and flaws, are more willing to accompany the character on an arc-journey for the duration of the book.

JUST AS OUR characters tend to grow by actively confronting obstacles through the course of a book, so do we grow as writers and humans by facing the challenges of developing strong characters with conscious and unconscious desires, strengths, weaknesses, and the potential for transformation.

4

QUAKELAND
—— Banish the Critic

E VEN THOUGH CRITICAL THOUGHTS HAVE ALWAYS
plagued me, particularly in my love life or when it came
to my appearance, in my writing life I've been relatively
successful in shutting out the creative critic. If I suffer rejection or disappointment I always manage to pick myself up
and get back to work. But I've learned to understand other
people's creative struggles by studying the harshest parts of
myself.

MY FIRST MUSE/BELOVED was Cat Stevens, which made
sense for a ten-year-old girl and a rock star. But even later,
I listened to my inner critic and actively ran away from real
Love and into the arms of emotional Pain. More than once.

In high school, a boy named Zane invited me over to his small stucco house in North Hollywood to work on a teenage suicide project for our sociology class.

Hazy carcinogenic smoglight of 1970s Los Angeles poured in through the leaves of the white-flowering magnolia trees outside as Zane put his *Ziggy Stardust and the Spiders from Mars* on the stereo.

"Listen to this," he said.

Trying to concentrate on teenage suicide, I was distracted by the long musculature of Zane's bicyclist's legs, his thick thatch of blond hair, tan skin, and eucalyptus leaf eyes. At that moment, I ignored all thoughts of death, though I had contemplated it before.

Zane had crushed on my friend Berry but she had no interest in him. I imagine it was just shyness, but people read her as cold. Because I looked nothing like Berry, with her dark skin and waist-length, shiny hair, her ice skater's thighs, I couldn't imagine that Zane would feel any attraction to me, even when he invited me into his room and asked to paint my portrait.

In my baby-blue sweatshirt, tight flared jeans, and Vans slip-ons, I sat on his twin bed and he squinted at me, putting acrylic paint on canvas. Maybe a beautiful boy would finally see me. And capture my image on canvas.

When I was twelve my father had me pose for him wearing a long shirt that covered my short shorts. In the photo, my eyes are downcast, my hair falling over my shoulders onto my chest, my limbs delicate and foal-like. Under his gaze my skin itched, as if burned by the sun that time when I was five; my mother had forgotten to apply sunscreen. The photo was never turned into the painting he'd promised, never joined the many images of my mother on the wall. By the time I was thirteen he had also stopped photographing me.

I don't remember much of what happened that last night with Zane, only the drive home in my rickety blue VW, the painting propped in the back seat. I wept so hard it was difficult for me to see the road. Oddly I remember the road more than almost anything else: the lights blurring through my tears, the strip malls, the steak house with metal plates and utensils that tanged the meat, where my family used to go until the body of a prostitute was found in a dumpster in the back.

I didn't return to Zane's house. We never saw each other again, though he sent me postcards from a cross-country bicycle trip he took after graduation.

Thinking of you. It's so peaceful here. Love, Zane.

Why did I run from him? What was I afraid of?

That I wasn't beautiful enough? That he would realize this and leave me? So I had to leave him first?

At an early age, I became my own worst critic. I'm still trying to understand why.

WHEN I WAS sixteen, my parents introduced me to their friend's son, twenty-year-old Johnny. I had been listening to

a Cat Stevens album when Johnny first came over with a
family friend. Maybe the lulling, romantic music, combined
with his dark green eyes, black hair, raggedly sensual lips, and
muscular, compact build, made me vulnerable. That, and the
fact that my parents seemed to love the idea of sending me
off with him to hike in the Hollywood Hills or watch him
rappel on Vasquez Rocks once a week.

Under the glass top of his desk he had hundreds of photographs of young women. Conveniently mute, I never said
a word about them. At a
party he took me to, directly
from a hike—my jeans and
hiking boots coated with
filth—I watched him flirt
with a blond girl in a clean

{ At an early age, I be-
came my own worst
critic. I'm still trying
to understand why. }

sundress and heels. After we left he told me he had to go back
"for something" and I waited in his VW Bug for him, knowing
the something was her phone number.

After a few months, my mother took me to get a dia-
phragm. I could almost see her clasping her hands with
delight when Johnny picked me up for a date, her eyes brim-
ming with proud tears. I'd never told her about the photos of
the women in his room or the party incident.

Johnny and his parents took me out to dinner for his
twenty-first birthday. We went to a steak house in Beverly Hills known for its expensive cuts of meat and salty,
sweet, spicy seasoning. We sat on the patio in the warm air
and stuffed ourselves with prime rib, but my body, used to

mostly vegetarian food at home, couldn't handle it. I felt thick with flesh.

Relieved not to be wearing my usual tight jeans, I had on a floral print, strapless sundress (not unlike the party girl's) that didn't constrict my expanded belly. The sun had streaked my hair, and I wore it blown back into feathered wings like Farrah Fawcett's. The sun had burned my skin; sometimes I got blisters from baking myself in baby oil.

Johnny and I said goodnight to his parents, and he drove me in his VW Bug to his English teacher's Spanish-style home in the Hollywood Hills. The house was decorated in muted tones and lit with candles, their reflections shining in the large plate glass windows overlooking the dark garden. I remember the large wooden bed, the white sheets and comforter, the high, firm mattress, but not the positions of our bodies or what anything felt like. Johnny snorted amyl nitrate when he came. It was the popular drug of choice for gay men in the seventies. His English teacher had given it to him.

Afterward Johnny noticed a fine hair growing near my aureole. "Get rid of that thing," he said. No one had told me that any part of my body was something to be ashamed of. Maybe I should have been grateful to him. I got some tweezers and plucked. And never faced that humiliation again.

Later I experienced a dull sense of contentment in my body (that came more from a certain pride at being the first of my close friends to lose my virginity than anything else) but not any actual pleasure, or pain either, save for the memory of that hair. We broke up a few weeks later. Except for one night of sobs, I was surprisingly unmoved. I had chosen him to reject me after all.

TOWARD THE END of senior year I met Hawk at Phases, a teen dance club at the far west end of the Valley where the air was greased with fast food and miles of darkness were punctured by bursts of fluorescence. This one large strobe-lit room with a dance floor surrounded by carpeted benches, a bar, and a pool table became our biweekly hangout. The DJ mostly played new wave but occasionally, especially on weeknights, he'd add punk bands to the mix.

A group of boys, slumping and scowling at the sidelines, would hurl themselves out onto the floor only when this music played. They wore jeans, combat boots, and T-shirts that said "Sick Pleasure" on them. As my friends Dirk, Elodie, Sasha, Berry, and I watched their crew, we knew that was what we wanted. That abandon, that sexuality, that darkness, that rough beauty. We named the leader with his sharp face and nasty smirk Rat; his sidekick in the plaid kilt, Little Italy; the cute, dumb one was Mole; and the sexy boy with the trench coat and pugnacious profile was Horse.

Hawk, who seemed to keep a little to himself, came up to me. He had a broken nose; a large, pale face; and a shaved head with a stiff crest of hair running down the center.

"You look like Jane Wiedlin," he told me.

The Go-Go's bassist! It was the highest compliment he could have given.

Then we were dancing like wild things, careening across the dance floor; he looked in my eyes and responded to my movements, unselfconscious about actually dancing *with* me.

The DJ announced a 1950s dance contest. "You want to enter?" Hawk asked. "The prize is a mirror," he laughed. "It's for snorting coke but we can just use it to put on eyeliner."

For the contest, I wore my mother's gold damask wedding dress. Hawk and I won the mirror that said "Phases" on it in silver lettering.

But instead of Hawk I asked another boy to the prom.

One night at Phases a pack of surreally tan, blond surfers arrived, flinging themselves onto the dance floor with us, twirling and tossing us like dolls; their teeth and the whites of their eyes glowed in the dark. Had they touched down from another planet? No, they lived a little ways north in Camarillo, a town famed for its mental hospital that supposedly inspired the Eagles song "Hotel California."

My friends and I went to a party there one night, exotic with our pink plaid kilts and ripped T-shirts and our mixed heritage (together we were black, Hispanic, Russian/Jewish, Polish—the Camarillo girls were all blond and blue-eyed like their boys, wearing cutoffs, white peasant blouses, and Vans).

Elodie, Sasha, Berry, and I drove home the next morning, the air overripe with strawberries and our heads moldered with the liquor punch.

I ended up asking one of these boys, Kewpie, to the prom. Maybe I thought he'd make a better impression on my classmates than Hawk. Maybe I was just torturing myself again.

My girlfriends' taffeta minidresses, and my own, matched the flamingo-pink Beverly Hills Hotel. (Dirk wore creepers and bondage pants and brought a petite girl with cropped hair, a satin cocktail dress, and a charming overbite.) We all arrived in a pink limo. Kewpie gave me bad cocaine on the mirror I'd won with Hawk, and we stormed the dance floor; wandered the damp, mossy gardens beneath the palm trees surrounding the hotel; and then went home to have sex on my parents' couch.

The next morning, sick with chills and fever, my throat scourged with pain, I made the mistake of showing my date a photograph of myself with my friends, including a girl named Marina whom he'd briefly dated before.

"She's so pretty," Kewpie said. "That smile, I think I might have been in love with her."

Typically, I'd picked the boy who would have chosen someone else, rather than the one who liked me and had the best hair.

BEFORE KEWPIE, HAWK, Johnny, and Zane, there was another boy, let's call him Gray. We'd been in the same "gifted" classes since first grade. At thirteen we stayed up talking on the phone late into the night. He told me about Little League, Jimi Hendrix, his lonely mother, his father's new wife, his little brother who had a life-threatening disease. I listened and tried to give some comfort. That was my role with all my friends. But this felt different. I liked this boy's intelligence, his small, sturdy, athletic body, his sad eyes.

One night he sounded a little out of it. I didn't know yet that he was high, that he would get high to kill his pain through most of junior high. That he would become addicted to cocaine and not get sober for many years. But that night, his words slurred. I don't remember the conversation, only one line that invaded through the phone wires, shaping everything that was to come.

"You'd be cute if someone cut off your head."

What provoked this brutality? Why did he say it? I had no idea.

The popular girls at my school were daughters of aspiring actresses and models; they had sun-bleached hair; thin, tan bodies; pearlish teeth; broad, high cheekbones; and the pale eyes of cats. They played tennis and got decent, but not too good, grades. One of them went on to grace the cover of *Cosmo*. These young goddesses wore pastel-colored skintight jeans, cotton T-shirts with lace inserts, and the highest version of the fawn suede cork platform Kork-Ease sandals I coveted.

{ Banish those critical voices. You have work to do. }

The day Gray decapitated me, I wore tight, high-waisted jeans, a tight French T-shirt with a small net insert embroidered with tiny flowers, and the low version of the popular suede platforms. But, of course, I was nothing like the popular girls.

I wasn't athletic; I got straight As. Mousy brown hair and pale skin already creased with worry lines across the brow. I can see my body, with sticklike limbs, developing breasts, and waist and hips of almost the same width, shambling around in that cute shirt, blood gushing from my neck, slayed by the critic.

THIRTY-FIVE YEARS LATER Gray ran into Zane.

"I think you know my ex-girlfriend, Francesca," Zane said. (He once considered me his girlfriend?)

"She was the first person to teach me about love," he added. (What did I teach this boy? That love hurts? That people leave out of fear? That I was a masochist who had made a big mistake? Or some tenderness I do not recall expressing?)

I learned all this because Gray found me on Facebook and came to my house with a gift—a book about a spiritual community in Findhorn where nature spirits are believed to live—to make amends for his cruelty. He was clean and sober, contrite. He even intimated that he'd had a crush on me in junior high, that he had read all my books since then, aloud to his ailing grandmother.

But the damage had already been deeply done. And the stage was set for my ultimate critic, Jaedon, though years would pass before he arrived.

"IF YOU HAVE ever considered taking your life go to the center of the circle," the teacher said. Her eyes were clouded from staring directly at the Pacific sunrise every morning, giving her an oracular appearance. "If you have never considered taking your life go to the perimeter of the circle."

At the "ecstatic dance" event, I watched as people huddled in the center of the floor, clutching their shoulders, eyes downcast. Others danced around them, swaying from side to side, holding up their hands to send "energy" to those in the middle.

Wrapped in burned velvet, I hovered somewhere between the two groups. I always had.

"Now pick a partner," the teacher said.

I turned, anxious, to see if anyone would join me. This was never my thing; I always worried I'd be the odd man out. And I felt extra vulnerable after the disturbing exercise.

No one acknowledged my presence.

Wanting to disappear, I tried to make my way off the dance floor when an older man stopped me and took my hand. Tall with scalding eyes. A Sinead O'Connor song played, and he began to move his long limbs, nuzzling his face into my hair and singing the lyrics in a tender voice. Soon I swooned into his arms. He lifted me in the air and spun me around as if I were weightless. It was the first time I'd felt I belonged here. Ecstatic dance, indeed.

"Jaedon," he said, at the end of class when everyone held hands in a circle and introduced themselves. His hand clasping mine felt big and warm, already familiar.

"I'd like you to come to this." He handed me a flyer for a yoga workshop he was leading. "I think I can help you."

A few days later, I lay prone in savasana, in a candlelit room, the air coated with the scent of wax and honey, while Jaedon put his hand on my belly. "You have some second chakra issues, yes?"

"I'm not sure," I said, conscious of the close proximity of his hand to my organs.

"Always giving to everyone. Digestive troubles. Maybe a little obsessive about sex. Low self-esteem."

I stiffened like the corpse I was imitating.

"It's okay," he reassured me. "You just need to be nurtured."

Jaedon took me to Electric Lotus in Los Feliz, where we ate Indian food among golden Buddhas, and electronic music made the table shake. Somehow the conversation turned back to my low self-esteem.

"Do you feel judged a lot?" Jaedon asked.

"The one thing I can't handle is someone judging my appearance," I said. I couldn't have set myself up better.

Jaedon squinted at me in the darkness. He had to raise his voice to be heard over the electronica. "I have to admit something to you. I'm judging your appearance right now."

"What? Why would you say that?" I jolted away from him.

"Don't be offended. It's just that you're very thin. And I was thinking, you look a little anorexic. I'm sorry. It's a thing for me."

"I'm not anorexic," I said. "I had some issues with that when I was much younger but not now."

Jaedon didn't seem to hear. "My grandmother was killed in a concentration camp. When my mother found out she lost her mind. It affected my childhood."

He showed me photographs he'd taken on a trip to Auschwitz. The pictures had somehow been double-exposed so that sketches of emaciated, screaming victims from an art exhibit he'd visited were superimposed over photos of the camp. The strangest picture: a neon sign ("Fresh Meat") mysteriously hovering over an image of an Auschwitz oven.

"I'm very disturbed by such extreme thinness," Jaedon said. "You can see why."

Disturbed or not, he continued to see me. And I continued to see him.

At a party at my house, Jaedon played drums and my friends and I danced. After everyone had left, Jaedon and I stood at my front window, staring through the candle flames reflected in the glass at the dark shadows obscuring the banana palms and birds of paradise.

"Your friend, Kali, she has a very strong sexual energy," Jaedon said.

I'd seen her grinning at him, flashing sharp incisors as she danced. A yoga teacher, too, with catlike features, long black hair, and tattoo-flower sleeves. Recently she'd adjusted my back in class and dislocated a rib. It still hurt when I took deep breaths. She'd offered me a free massage as an apology.

"Why are you telling me that, Jaedon?" I said.

"It shouldn't bother you. You're who I'm seeing. You're who I want."

Again, he wasn't the only one to blame. Why had I introduced him to Kali? Why had I invited her over after the rib incident? Why was I still with him at all?

The next morning I had a photo shoot for the *Times*. The final pictures showed my eyes dazed and swollen from crying the night before. The photos also revealed that something had gone wrong with the rhinoplasty I'd had a few years prior. The bones at the tip of my nose had slipped, causing an irregular slant. I stared in horror at the final shots. *This is what Jaedon sees, this is why he's said what he's said.*

But the final humiliation came on a hike in the mountains. Jaedon suggested we sit at the side of the trail and eat our lunch. Afterward, he began to kiss me. I felt uncomfortable, exposed out there in the harsh sun, where anyone could walk by, but I let him. Soon his hands were down my pants. While he touched me inside, so deeply it felt like he could reach in and pull out a part of me, he stared into my face and said, "I'm glad you aren't too attractive. Otherwise you might be too much of a distraction."

I slithered away from him, clutching my belly. "I have to leave," I said.

It felt like hours before we reached the trailhead. When I got home I had received an email from my publisher. I'd won a lifetime achievement award from the American Library Association.

THIS WAS THE moment when things changed. I looked at the photographs from the *Times* and saw not a monster, but an insecure woman who'd been convinced by a former therapist to have cosmetic surgery.

I looked at Jaedon and saw an angry, wounded man with a history of hate and pain. He was, I realized, just another aspect of myself.

I broke up with him the next day. A month later I traveled to Chicago and my publisher escorted me to a ballroom filled with hundreds and hundreds of empty seats.

"What's this for?" I asked.

"That's where you'll be making your speech. Everyone is coming to hear you."

Incomprehensible. Still in my early forties and dressed in California casual—a saltwater pearl and peach crystal necklace from my editor, a white gauze tunic from the Hare Krishna temple store, white linen flared jeans with gold thread trim, and copper metallic wedges—I didn't look or feel like the recipient of a lifetime achievement award from a major institution.

But I didn't feel undeserving, either. As my father had said, I was a writer. And my body (thin skin, fragile nerves, small frame, and all), as well as my writer's mind, had worked hard to produce books that touched people. At least for a while, I didn't involve myself with any more Jaedons, critics who simply verbalized the secret thoughts that already existed inside my brain.

ALTHOUGH NO VILE inner *creative* critic lurks within me, I've still experienced many challenges with my writing. One online reviewer commented on my author photo, mentioning my "too long" nose and "long skinny face" masked by "too much makeup" as well as the nipples showing through my grandmother's antique lace wedding dress.

"She wasn't beautiful," this critic proclaimed, "at least not in any traditional sense of the word." The photo had been hard for me to take—literally. I'd forced myself to do it, relying on a makeup artist to cover the acne scars on my skin and a photographer to soften my features with shadow. Even sometimes to this day, I experience physical pain when I think of this "review."

A Christian group in Minnesota petitioned to have one of my books—a 120-page coming-out, coming-of-age fairy tale—burned, like a little witch at the stake, for its homosexual content, and a man with a Rumpelstiltskin beard railed about the book's sinful nature in an online video.

The novel I wrote about Jaedon received a rejection from my publisher and a remark that she found the characters "distasteful." My agent at the time informed me of this one day as I walked my dogs Vincent Van Go-Go Boots and Thumper on the purple jacaranda sidewalks around the park where I'd raised my children.

"But my readers need to read about this part of my life, too," I told her. "They need to know the shadow side is real."

After a very brief period of "mourning," I extensively rewrote and expanded the book and published it elsewhere. Even then, some found it hard to stomach. One review was so scathing that the newspaper pulled it, though another reviewer lauded the book for portraying one of the most reprehensible villains she'd ever read, and others commented on the meta aspects and the densely lyrical writing. Neither the negative nor positive responses really mattered though. What mattered is that I'd told the story of Jaedon,

> Neither the negative nor positive responses really mattered. What mattered is that I'd told the story.

and had the opportunity to share it with others as well. Maybe some young woman might benefit from what had happened to me.

Years later, I received a message from a young gazelle with waist-length waves of hair and nerd-chic glasses that framed long-lashed eyes and rested perfectly on high, rounded cheekbones. She asked if she could work as my intern, and from the first moment I met her it was as if she'd walked out of one of my novels. Except, unlike my characters, she knew how to expertly file, organize, and work with numbers!

One day we were sharing our dating experiences and I asked her, "Where'd you learn how to be so poised and smart with men?"

"From your books," she said.

SOMETIMES WE SUFFER from the lacerations and flagellations of gargoyles telling us that what we're writing is flawed, ugly, unlovable. It's easy to fall prey to these beasts.

Anne Lamott suggests you pick up your critical inner voices by the tail like rats and put them in a mason jar, fasten the lid, turn down the volume, and watch them scratch away, well contained.

As you did with your muse, try to imagine how your inner critic looks, sounds, feels, and even maybe smells and tastes, depending on the intimacy of your relationship. Are your muse and your critic related in any way? What wound motivates the critic? What does he want? What does she need? What is his gift? Her flaw? Does this inner judge serve any purpose for you? What do you believe about what they have to say? Do you consciously agree with any of it?

Talk back to this angry, undermining part of yourself. If you send your critic to a good therapist and then let him put on an editor's hat for a little while, he can help you when you're revising your work. But for now, banish those critical voices. We have work to do.

THE 12 QUESTIONS: ANTAGONIST
Question #6: Who are your character's antagonists?

ANTAGONISTS ARE ESSENTIAL. To grow, a character needs an antagonist to interfere with the character's quest to get what he wants, and by doing so, force him to achieve what he needs.

An antagonist needs to be a person, as opposed to a concept or event (such as global warming or war, for example) or an internal struggle (such as self-doubt). These situations and struggles can exist on their own but also become externalized through the antagonist.

The antagonist must be a **dimensional character**. Applying the first four questions to the antagonist as well as the protagonist will help you to infuse your antagonist with her own needs and wants. If your antagonist isn't fully coming to life, try writing sections of your story from the antagonist's point of view. They may not make it into your final book, but the exercise will add layers of substance.

The antagonist is an external expression of the story's problem. Just as there are many kinds of problems, there can be many kinds of antagonists, such as:

The **"big bad"** antagonist: This character is otherwise known as the "villain" or the "heavy." He must be complex and dimensional, not a mustache-twirling caricature. Often, the reader will glean the lesson the main character needs by observing the negative actions of a big bad antagonist.

The **"false antagonist"** is the character who is perceived as a real antagonist to keep the tension in the story high. In a mystery, a false antagonist can also distract the reader, and the main character, from the true antagonist by serving as a red herring. This can also work in novels that are not traditional mysteries but have page-turning elements.

The **"loving antagonist"** has the main character's best interest at heart but often stands in the way of her want. Often the reader will see the thing that the main character needs to learn expressed through the positive actions of this antagonist.

In *To Kill a Mockingbird*, Mr. Ewell is the **big bad antagonist**, a closed-minded racist whom Scout must overcome to reach the climax of her story. Boo Radley is the **false antagonist**, seen as threatening at first but ultimately heroic. Atticus is, at times, a **loving antagonist** in that he forces Scout to change and mature.

Tom Buchanan and George Wilson are the **big bads**, the antagonists who ultimately destroy Gatsby. Daisy is his **loving antagonist**, the one who inspires him to become something new, even though that new Gatsby is ultimately unsuccessful.

There are also **primary** and **secondary** antagonists:

In *Jane Eyre*, Rochester is a **primary antagonist**, while Jane's aunt and cousins are **secondary antagonists**.

In *Wuthering Heights*, Hareton—Catherine's jealous, cruel brother—is Heathcliff's **primary antagonist**, along with Catherine. Catherine is a **primary loving antagonist**.

In *Lolita*, Clare Quilty, the pornographer who kidnaps Lolita and is murdered by Humbert, is the **primary antagonist**—Humbert's most overt nemesis.

In *Play It As It Lays*, Maria's director husband, Carter, is the **primary antagonist**, while her friends BZ and Helene are **secondary antagonists**.

The people who push us out of our comfort zones are the ones who make us grow the fastest. By exploring characters based on these challenging friends, lovers, and foes, you will have more dimensional antagonists in your book, and more challenges for your protagonist to conquer. At the same time, this process will give you, the writer, an opportunity to better understand and navigate difficult relationships in your own life.

> Creating powerful sensory descriptions can have a healing effect on the writer.

WRITING ABOUT ANTAGONISTS also gives you yet another chance to better understand yourself, as the greatest antagonist is usually the one who lies within.

THE HEALING LANGUAGE OF METAPHOR

The language of metaphor can create an emotional connection with a reader.

A person who suffers great loss felt might feel as if his heart is literally breaking. And he might use this expression to convey his feelings to another person, and to feel less alone in the world.

But truths of this nature—*my heart is breaking*—are so true that they have become clichés, and it is our job to find fresh and new ways to evoke this same universal feeling.

Many of my own metaphors describe heartache, perhaps because that is the feeling that I most want to define and share. Heartaches can't always be contained in literal words; we need comparisons to show painful, dramatic experiences.

A few months ago, while I was deep into the writing of a book, Secret Man told me that I seemed preoccupied, unavailable. He was right: My focus was deeply intent on the book I was creating.

After I thought about it for a while, I came up with this metaphor to help him understand what I was going through:

"I feel like a starving lioness who's just killed a deer and she's got to feed it to her hungry cubs. It's all she can think about. But it's just for right now. Once I've filled up a little I'll be able to pay attention to the lion, too."

My faithful Leo seemed to understand and accept the situation much more easily after that.

A few weeks later, I was preoccupied again, this time with my low bank balance. While I worried, two gray doves were building a messy, fragile nest flat on the ground where possums, raccoons, and cats could decimate it. The female dove ran in circles, haphazardly tossing twigs and rotten leaves into the mix.

"I feel like those doves," I said to Secret Man. "Like the nest is going to fall apart or the eggs are going to be eaten."

He understood, and reassured me that I was safe. "You're a very good nest builder," he said. ⸻

CREATING POWERFUL SENSORY descriptions can have a healing effect on the writer as well. Descriptions of food might make my readers hungry, but for me the sensuality of writing about food—the taste, the scent, the ingredients— helped me to heal my struggles with eating by reminding me of its magical, life-giving aspects.

5

THE FRENZY
—— Chaos into Order

Growing up in a land that quakes makes you naturally anxious.

Especially when you live in a stilted home.

Well, my childhood house didn't really perch on stilts like those homes that used to hover on the cliffs of Mulholland Drive; our home nestled on a shady street, across from a gulley on the Valley side of Laurel Canyon. But at times my life felt precarious even there.

On February 9, 1971, the earth shuddered. My brother called out to me in the middle of the night: "Get up!"

"I can't," I said, from my shaking bed.

He rushed to my side, imagining me pinned down by fallen beams—he told me later—and carried me into the living room. Bits of broken glass covered the floor and my dog, the cock-a-poo Teddy, shook like a little earthquake himself. My father packed us all up in the Volvo station wagon and drove us to a motel out of town. We returned the next day and pretended nothing had happened but I think it always affected us—creating an awareness of the fault lines in our psyches.

The second big earthquake I lived through: Smoke and I were staying at my childhood home and awoke to the bed sliding across the room. After we'd cleaned up the debris, we went over to his mother's house where his blond baby nieces, Tweetie Sweet Pea and Peachie Pie, crouched on the floor meticulously picking up shards of glass from the fallen family portraits until their grandmother found them and sent them away from the danger zone.

My brother's friend's elderly mother was killed by a piece of furniture in that Northridge quake of 1994. My own mother, without my father to distract and comfort her, lived in mortal terror of the next catastrophe.

Even without the threat of earthquakes marrowed in my bones, I come by my anxiety, my fear of and perverse attraction to chaos—just as I come by my writing abilities—honestly.

MY GRANDMOTHER, A writer herself, endured electroshock therapy for her mood disorder. My poetic mother fell deeper and deeper into panic after my father was diagnosed with cancer. Later, she exhibited hoarding tendencies.

"My boxes, my boxes," my mother moaned. "What will I do with them? I have to go through them. When I do I'll be able to take Tai Chi and dance again. I'll be able to visit you more." But she never went through her boxes. They crammed her apartments—she brought them with her everywhere she moved; there was barely room to walk across the floor.

"She just needed someone to help her," My Secret Man said when I told him.

After she died I tried to absorb much of what she had left behind into my already cluttered home. But it only made my own anxiety worse. The more things you have, the more things can break. The more places ghosts can hide. The more you have to lose.

"I WANT TO live in a room with white walls, a few pieces of white wooden furniture, and wood floors," I told Secret Man, soon after we got together. "Nothing else. Except the kids." *And you.*

"Then why don't you?" he asked.

His hair, cut like David Bowie's in the nineties, auras his face with silver. At fifty-seven, his face exudes youth. Everyone says his eyes are kind. One of them has an enlarged pupil like Bowie's, both the result of childhood injuries. Because my beau's eyes are so dark, from his half-Spanish heritage, it's not as apparent as Bowie's, unless I look very closely.

We sat on the couch, a gray-green velvet island in a living room crowded with my dead mother's artifacts, my dead father's paintings, my old books. A fine dust—the pollen of crumbled paper and leather and dried rose petals and powdery earth from a sacred site—coated everything. Maybe it was why My Secret had been coughing so much.

My home wasn't always this way. When I moved in eight years ago, the rooms, walls, and floors were bare. A man I dated briefly told me once, "You're the warmest thing in here." It wasn't meant as a compliment.

In college, my boyfriend, Thorn, gave me a psychological quiz.

"You enter a white room without anything in it. How do you feel?"

"Calm," I said.

"The white room is death," he told me.

My father was dying then; I had turned my own body skeletal; I wanted death.

But now, thirty years later, I wanted the tranquility of nearly empty rooms in which to *live*.

MY SECRET CAN manipulate space to serve its best purpose. I, on the other hand, put one shoe in the box and then move the second one around in the air a few times to figure out how it fits. "Spatially challenged," I call it.

Maybe I just need to slow down and concentrate the way I do when I write. I read once that girls who struggle with math often have fraught relationships with their fathers; perhaps some kind of anxiety about the abstract world develops?

"I'll help you," My Secret Man said. "If you want."

"Yes."

A week later we began. He came over on his day off; I worried that he would resent it eventually, spending his free time this way. Going through my things. Secret seeing all

{ I come by my perverse attraction to chaos—and my writing—honestly. }

my secrets. My dirt, my dark corners. That the disturbed dust would make him cough more. But he reassured me. "I'll tell you if it gets to be too much."

We started with my books. I can arrange words on a page but I can't seem to organize books on a shelf. Over the years, My Secret has shelved thousands and thousands, held each one in his hands. He thinks they might have seeped into him, through his skin, as much as the books he's read. At night and on his days off we spend hours talking about writing. He reads three or four books at a time. When he's not working at the bookstore he goes to other bookstores around the city and browses until closing time. Holding more volumes in his hands, filling himself up with words.

I'd placed all my books on two small bookcases, double layered them on the small shelves. We pulled them from the bookcase, one by one; I handed him those I felt ready to relinquish, put the "maybes" on a shelf in front of us, piled the yeses on top. When unsure, I looked at him; he watched me calmly and with his full attention. *I am here.*

My dog, Elphi, dropped his toy into an empty box and started digging frantically trying to get it back out. We retrieved it for him and he repeated.

"He's trying to help us," My Secret said.

FOR YEARS AFTER both Vincent Van Go-Go Boots and Thumper had died, my daughter begged me to get another dog.

"I could barely take care of Vincent and Thumper in the end," I said.

"You did a great job of taking care of them, Mommy," she reassured me. Then: "Except for the part where you killed them."

Great.

Her strategy worked, though, and one night, after dreaming of a buffalo with dreadlocks collapsing heavily on his side to let me stroke his belly, I drove by the animal shelter and my friend Ez suggested we go inside. At the back in a cage piled with smaller dogs, I spotted a long-haired slinkster being savaged by a brute with an under bite. I hesitated but Ez said, "I wonder if he's the buffalo in your dream?"

Elphi blearily tried to lick my face when I held him in my arms. The deal was sealed when I noticed the way the fur on his ears had twisted into dreadlocks just like my dream buffalo's. As we left the shelter, down a corridor of moaning pit bulls and German shepherds, he trotted along like a circus animal, oblivious to the threat around him, though on our walks at home he still lunges at these breeds (and anything with an under bite) as if in delayed self-defense.

Eventually, now, Elphi settled against My Secret Man's hip. Warmth radiated off of both of them, reassuring me while Bowie sang about leaving this life, traveling light. I want that, also: to be able to put everything important into my car and leave at a moment's notice, in case of disaster.

Fire, flood, earthquake. When I die, I don't want my kids to be burdened with my crap. My brother Zack and I spent days at my mother's last apartment, throwing boxes and boxes into dumpsters; he took carloads to Out of the Closet. So much was still left.

We filled my garage, floor to ceiling, with her books—those that belonged to her and to my father and her father. Coffee table art books of Vermeer and Picasso and Rembrandt, novels and poetry volumes with leather covers and onion skin sheaths over the illustrations, defunct encyclopedias. Book dealers came over to look at them, picked through, found almost nothing except one signed copy of a lesser-known F. Scott Fitzgerald that I sold to pay my mortgage that month.

Now, I only keep books for teaching, a few other novels and poetry books, very little else.

"I can always get you new, clean copies," My Secret said. "Any time."

Five ancient, leatherbound illustrated French books with dark green or dark blue marbled paper trim contain drawings by the artist Watteau, commedia del arte characters reclining in pastoral settings; hand-colored pictures of elegant ladies and gents with the heads of pigs, goats, horses, birds; drawings of girls with flower faces. Wilting tulip girls. A rose in a vase with a human face. The moon regarding herself in a lake; in another drawing she reclines on a cloud looking down at the sun. A weird ballerina with elongated feet. I think she resembles me. An illustration called "Apocalypse du Ballet" where fairies dance with bodyless stockinged gnomes.

(My Secret Man will carry these from his store to a seller of rare books downtown. He will not be there. My Secret Man will walk back with the heavy books still in tow. He will go again another day. The bookseller will say the books are "cripples" not worth anything except one, which Secret will sell to him for me. The others we'll give to an artist who shows her work in the gallery above the bookstore; maybe she'll use them in a collage. With the money, I will insist on buying Secret pumpkin curry at our favorite vegan Thai place and a thick cotton hoodie to keep him warm, since he's given me both of his.)

After the books, we carried heavy pieces of my mother's dark furniture onto the porch to donate to the Vietnam Vets—plant stands of inlaid wood, a table with ironwork roses, a hope chest filled with sewing supplies, carved Italian chairs with embossed leather seats.

Then we moved to my desk heaped with folders of my class plans, original manuscripts with editor's notes, tax receipts. He sat with me while I sorted through them, tossed most into the recycle bin. Put the remainder in folders in a drawer he helped me empty of stationery I never used. Old speakers had been tucked away underneath the desk. Boxes of cables that belonged to lost, broken, or misplaced devices. He looked through them quickly, tossed them in the trash. I watched, feeling as if I'd pulled a plug to a running machine. Sparks flying. Fear of shock. *What if I need those things?*

"You won't need these things," he said. "There'll be more room to think. And write."

We got rid of two broken keyboards (one with a missing *8 key and one with an @2 key that sent off a string of expletives) and he ordered me a new one off the Internet. The stationery I did keep, he tucked neatly into a small basket that fit perfectly on the desk shelf. He has an eye for what will fit where. Once, when he was working in a shoe store in Hawaii, a Feng Shui master saw him stacking boxes with such grace and precision she asked him to come work for her.

When I walked into this house the first time, into the sun-filled room that smelled of fresh, white paint, I found the built-in shelves especially charming. Small containers within the larger container of the home. A way to organize my messy life. I'd since cluttered them with dried-rose-wreathed Buddhas and Quan Yins; Shiva and Krishna and Ganesh and Saraswati; chunks of amethyst and rose quartz; glass vases with peacock feathers inside; my dog Vincent Van Go-Go Boots's ashes. The cedar box with the lock reminds me that when our other dog, the pitbull/beagle mix, Thumper, died, I didn't have the resources, financial or emotional, to bring home a box of her remains.

THE FIRST TIME Thumper seized, her body flung itself about as if possessed. Pee and shit splashed and spattered the walls. Afterward she growled and snapped, not recognizing me. I worried she would hurt my children.

My neighbor came to take them out for pizza while I cleaned up, the dog confined in a room until she recovered.

My son, only five at the time, refused to leave. He stood guard by my side, jaw tense, eyes alert.

"He's such a mama's boy," my neighbor said.

But I knew better and said so. "He's trying to protect me."

"I'm okay, Sammy," I promised. I couldn't say the same about our dog.

Guilt still clutches at me. And shakes.

My ex-husband and I had found her on the street a few years before, running along with frantic determination. We stopped the car and called her to us. She had a collar with a tag—but it was blank. Vincent Van Go-Go Boots, the springer spaniel, took one look at her and love blossomed. They lay side by side all day and she methodically licked the cauliflower cyst on his eye. Once, she ran away and came back a short time later, standing at the front door with a fully cooked and ready-to-serve ham delivered to us from her mouth. I always like to imagine the look on the faces of the people whose dinner she stole.

When Vincent had died, a vet came to my house and I held my springer in my arms while medicine was administered. My mother, brother, and boyfriend at the time, the Brazilian photographer Mateus, surrounded me. Afterward, Vincent's ashes were delivered to me in the polished wood box. But things had changed. A year later, I was struggling financially. My mom was in Ojai, pining over her current lover and experiencing the early, undiagnosed (she refused to reveal them to my brother or me or go to a doctor) symptoms that would later be linked to the cancer that killed her.

My boyfriend Mateus had broken up with me. After a series of expensive tests and medicine that didn't work, Thumper still seized regularly.

I drove to the vet alone in the rain. My dog's body looked sleek, muscular, strong, and healthy. Only her lopsided face with the bony, protruding skull and strange eyes showed signs that something was wrong.

The vet asked me to leave the room. "It'll be hard to watch this."

I didn't hold her in my arms. I watched her trot away. I still taste death in my mouth and feel it leaden in my gut when I think of what I had to do. *What if she bit my children after a seizure?* I keep reminding myself. It doesn't help.

A short time later my kids, who had already been through the death of two dogs, one cat, and two goldfish, lost their grandmother. The chaos that ensued after her passing infiltrated all aspects of my life, from my relationships to my health to my house, which became a jumbled mess; nothing could be seen clearly. Nothing felt safe.

You did a great job of taking care of them, Mommy. Except for the part where you killed them.

I SHOWED MY Secret Man the box of ashes and the peacock feathers in the vase, and he shuddered, almost imperceptibly, at the animal detritus. His response to the ashes made sense, but I'd forgotten that he dislikes birds after an experience with a woman who left him alone in a room with a murderous parrot (though My Secret Man seems to remember everything I've ever told him about myself).

When I'd put the peacock feathers in the vase, had I forgotten that I don't like birds either? The peacock feathers had belonged to my mother; those long, stringy strands of iridescence littered the house where I'd grown up. My father liked to paint them.

I had a friend, Valentine, who lived in Beachwood Canyon. The cigarettes in her ashtray had gold tips on one end and, on the other, crimson lipstick stains the color of her hair. She slept with the television on so as not to hear the peacocks screaming in her garden.

> I was done worshipping at the shrine of pain.

Valentine also had a parrot that perched on a post in her room.

"He'll be fine," she said, leaving me there with him, just as My Secret's friend had done. "He doesn't like to be put in his cage. Don't worry."

The parrot rolled its eyes at me, cackling obscenities, the whole time Valentine was gone.

Peacocks, parrots, and pigeons make me shudder, too, and not imperceptibly. I guess I'd forgotten.

Or, somehow, kept the peacock feathers there simply because they'd been in my parents' house.

I realized that so many of my choices feel like a betrayal of myself.

Three dark paintings by my father—two self-portraits and a picture of a kneeling, bald monk in a dark robe, brooded on the shelves.

"Do you mind if we move these?" My Secret Man asked. "The energy is really dark." He seemed to be able to read each item in my home.

He held one painfully small gold bracelet in his palm for a moment, considering its secrets, and then, with slightly less of a shudder than the one the feathers garnered, suggested I sell it.

It must make life hard sometimes, this gift. Hearing the voices of that many ghosts.

When we first started dating, Secret Man admired the framed picture of my mother laughing on a swing in Jamaica on the cruise my brother took us on after my father, his stepfather, died. Her teeth show, her blond hair flies back. The frame is silver irises, daffodils, and rabbits. Spring.

"How old is she here?" My Secret Man had asked me.

"My age."

"Oh, wow," he'd said.

"What does that mean? Do I look a lot older than she did?" People had often thought we were sisters.

"No, she just looks very beautiful."

I'd always been lost in the blaze of her light. I had tried to explain it. "Everyone's been telling me how beautiful she is for my whole life."

"Then why don't you take the picture down?"

I'd never even considered the possibility.

My life had been a shrine to her, even before she died, even when I was a little girl, her likeness, painted by my father, covering every wall of our house.

I took the photo down and put it in the garage.

That was the first time the room sighed in ages. It used to reverberate with breath, like my rib cage when I danced in the living room. I hadn't done that for years, until just the other night.

"Let's dance," My Secret had said.

We moved together for a while, eyes closed, palms pressed to palms.

"Now I want to see you dance."

He sat on the couch and I reeled around, dropped to the floor at his feet, rolled and stretched. Sia's "Breathe Me" playing.

"That was so beautiful," he said, as I lay panting and lightly shined with sweat, on his chest, his heart thudding in my ears. "You should dance more."

HE HELPED ME clean the rest of the mantel and the built-in shelves. We put most of what was on them in a box for the Vietnam Vets. He piled everything carefully, in perfect balance.

We moved my books to the case that'd been mostly emptied. He stood and squinted at the bare shelves, then carefully placed a few select things back. An oil painting my father had done of me as a baby next to a similarly pastelled photo of my daughter at the same age. Blue tiles with my children's baby handprints. One blue Delft vase; one pink and green glass vase; two rose quartz Quan Yins from my mother; an amethyst crystal. Photo albums of my babies' faces. For years

I only took close ups of them, nothing else, sometimes put four or five versions of the same exact shot next to each other in the album.

"This is what my life is about," I told him. "My children. My books. That's all really."

You. The rest are deceased things.

"I know," he said, moving the two Quan Yins to another shelf. Tenderly adjusting their angles. They have robes that look like silk when light shines through them, even though they are made of stone. Everything in its perfect place. Only the colors I love (rose quartz, white, touches of jade, amethyst, Krishna-blue, Delft-blue) were allowed to stay, part of his selection process.

He watches me closely—what I wear, what I'm drawn to. He listens and remembers.

He put a small portrait of my brother, and one of me, on either end of the mantel. I would have put them facing in, facing each other, but My Secret had them facing out, looking out toward their separate lives, but not too far apart if they needed each other.

We piled the discards on the porch. Half the room done. Then, time for lunch at the place we went on our first date. My appetite, suppressed for months, came back as I ate the buckwheat crust pizza slathered with pesto sauce and vegetables, topped with creamy green avocado. We even shared a raw coconut and fresh vanilla bean milkshake.

He asked, "Do you like your house? Do you think it will make it easier for you to write?"

"No one's ever done anything this nice for me before," I said.

It was only the beginning.

ON THE SECOND day, he asked, "Do you want help with your house again?"

He came over and pulled some cash from my sold books out of his pocket. In this way he's teaching me that it pays to let go. But I've seen it already; all week I worked better at my desk, didn't cringe walking past my bookshelves. My brain clear of those decimated pages and disintegrating, silently shrieking peacock feathers.

We started in on the other half of the living room. A white wooden shelf unit, scavenged from my alley, crammed with CDs, DVDs, VHS tapes, cassette tapes. We sat on the floor and he picked out the few CDs he thought we could sell. Tori, PJ, Patti, Bjork, Prince, Iggy, Bowie. They're all on my computer by now anyway. I put aside my children's baby-favorites to store in the garage. The cassette tapes I threw in the trash, including those that warbled with recordings of my mother crying to my dead father.

The more difficult task came in the form of an Art Nou-veau cherry wood cabinet lined with pink velvet. On its glass shelves sat a hundred small items. From my maternal grandparents: a yarmulke and prayer shawl, a silver chalice for the Angel Elijah to drink from, tiny framed photos of my grandparents frolicking in the waves in old-fashioned swim suits and caps. He's thin, high-cheek-boned, balding, swarthy—Sephardic. She's pale, mouse-haired with heavier features. Not like my mother whose hair was white blond, naturally Marilyn, turning to a more burnished gold in her thirties. Whose face had a lighter cast.

I look more like the grandmother who had received electroshock treatments for anxiety and depression, who supported her family with her writing; she had to move alone to Hollywood to the Garden of Allah, the hotel with the pool in the shape of the red sea, where movie stars like Clark Gable and Lana Turner, and even writers like F. Scott Fitzgerald, lived. (Maybe that's where she got the signed copy!)

My mother and grandfather joined her later. But my mom wanted to stay back east with her gentle father. Observing the habits of butterflies, bees, and ants in the countryside. Having him all to herself.

I guess I wanted the same thing, but my father was too obsessed with my mother to pay much attention.

From him, in the case: a gold watch face, a raw silk tie striped gem-blue and gem-green, an ancient iridescent Egyptian glass vessel used to collect mourner's tears for tombs, bronze sculptures of the heads of women resembling my mother—my father had made them progressively thinner and thinner until they recalled the anorexic work of the sculptor Giacometti. Women fading into nothingness.

From my mother: a cloth doll she'd made me. It has her blond (yarn) hair and green (embroidered) eyes. "I should have made her dark like you," she said with sudden insight just before she died. "How self-centered."

From my child self: a celluloid baby doll in a wooden carriage nosed by a small stuffed lamb. A round box covered with roses and full of handmade doll clothes. A Penny Wooden from London in a black velvet dress decorated with pearl buttons. A bisque-faced doll with golden braids and blushed cheeks and painted on lashes. Her feet are cloth, overstuffed with straw, bulbous and rotting inside her lace socks. Her china hands must have first belonged to a baby doll, much too small for her.

An assortment of tiny china dolls with real human hair, glass eyes, and jointed limbs that swing uselessly from their sockets.

I've had an obsession with dolls ever since childhood. Surrounded myself with effigies of babies, as if trying to conjure my future children into being. When we first met I showed My Secret pictures of Isla de la Muñecas in Mexico. It's a man-made island where a hermit lived. He found the corpse of a girl and her doll on the shore and strung the doll in a tree to appease the girl's spirit. Still, ghosts wailed, waking him in the night.

Over the years he collected hundreds and hundreds of dolls and hung them everywhere. Their heads on posts, their bodies dangling from branches. Hollow, plastic-lidded eyes and pursed lips revealing seed-pearl-sized teeth. Dirt-scrubbed cheeks. Cobwebbed hair like ratted nests. Clowns and babies and Barbies and mermaids crawling with caterpillars, greened with moss, painted red like blood.

My Secret and I can't afford a vacation now; my house will have to do. We filled box upon box with my dead things and he carried them to the porch. We put the Art Nouveau curio cabinet in the alley for the neighborhood scavengers.

(The next morning I will go out to look for it, regretting my decision—those elegant lines, that polished wood. It will be gone. I will learn that part of this purging process is regret. That it is to be expected and accepted, a sign that one has done the work.)

We carried the dollhouse I ostensibly bought for my daughter, but really for myself, to house the collection of doll furniture I've collected since childhood, into the garage. (Something I'm not ready to give away. A little house, a controlled world from before I had learned to navigate my larger world.)

We brought my pale yellow drop-leaf desk in from the garage. The roses on it, hand-painted with eight light-pink dabs, five shaded darker pink inside around one darker center, bloom among festoons of green leaves and pale blue paint-brushed blossoms. He put the desk where the curio cabinet had been.

"I think this is kind of cool," he said. His voice had a tender creak. "This is where you wrote your first book."

The discarded items are better kept as words, anyway, I told myself. But in the night I heard the sound of crying and got up to retrieve the china dolls and the rose-covered box and my father's watch. The big doll now has a place on the shelf next to the Egyptian vessel shaped like a teardrop. The smaller dolls belong in the rose box on my hand-painted desk. I gave the watch to my son, Sam, hoping my ancestors' spirits would be appeased with these concessions.

And with the idea that maybe I'll have more space in which to write their stories after I've thrown or given almost everything else away.

ON THE THIRD day, My Secret and I ventured into my bedroom.

"It won't be that bad," I said.

He remained quiet. He didn't seem so sure. Later he'd tell me, "Closets are the worst." But he didn't want to say it in advance, frighten me from the task.

I dragged everything out; stacks of boxes covered the entire floor of my room, clothes submerged the bed. Bowie was blasting "live": *Reality Tour*, making me brave, keeping us calm. My Secret doesn't love clutter.

"As a kid my father made me clean out abandoned houses with him, haul away other people's trash," he said.

That can't have been easy for a twelve-year-old boy. I recognized, even more, the value of this gift.

I sat on the floor with him next to me as I sorted through boxes of photographs. "You're doing great, lover," he said.

These photos are of the halcyon baby days when my marriage was intact, my children new and unscarred by the divorce to come. In one photo, I sit on the bed with my three-month-old and two-year-old in my arms. My face is glowing and peaceful, my breasts, in a tight camisole, full with milk; I never felt so beautiful, so fulfilled.

I kept almost all the pictures. But then I found some that a plastic surgeon took after he fixed my nose. It was round like my father's to begin with and had been broken when I was six—my friend's brother, who I thought was cute, ran into me head-on with a toy gun.

The doctor never really fixed the problem. He used cartilage from inside my nose to construct a squared-off tip unnatural to my face and Eastern European heritage. Eventually I had to have four more hours of surgery by two different doctors to try to correct the damaged interior and the uneven exterior.

In these pictures my nose still looks good. My face looks pretty, so ridiculously young. But I seem deered-in-the-headlights. The pain when they pulled out the packing in my nostrils seared worse than the natural childbirth I'd later endure.

"You should throw those away," My Secret Man said. It was the only time he'd said this. I realized it was because he knew the story, he didn't want me to keep something so clearly associated with pain.

At first I think my insecurities scared him; he wasn't sure how they might wound us both. But he'd told me, "I understand now. You just need to be reassured. I think you should only spend time with people who reassure you. Doctors, friends."

You, I think. The one who told me, that day I got so triggered by the comment about my beautiful mother: "I prefer your looks to hers." It was all I needed.

I hesitated about throwing the pictures away but I did anyway, along with dilapidated shoeboxes and molting angel wings made of real feathers. Those pictures will be the only things I think of going into the trash to retrieve the next day. But I don't.

> My grandmother's dark pink silk
> kimono embroidered with giant
> peonies. My aunt's evening gown
> of mesh lace embroidered with se-
> quin blossoms that I wore to punk
> clubs as a teenager. My mother's
> dress of gold damask that I wore
> to win a 1950s dance contest with
> the sweet punk boy I then stupidly
> rejected for the coke-head surfer.
> All this needed to go. *I'll write*
> *about them*, I told myself.

We stuff the better clothes into plastic trash bags to sell. A pair of sheer Pucci pants, a rose silk Tahari dress, a silk baby doll dress in paisley pink and green, a vintage pink beaded mesh top, a Helmut Lang white denim jacket, a kid's dark denim Levi's jacket that I could fit into at nineteen after I'd stopped eating. Christian Louboutin hot-pink sandals with those red soles, gifts from my former agent, that contributed to the arthritis in my toe joints like shoes in a fairy tale. Prada leopard-print Lucite sandals that made my feet bleed when I jumped up and down in them on a date with a man who fucked me at night but pretended he didn't know me during the day. Six-inch black platforms and turquoise suede platforms that look like Bowie would have worn them in the seventies. I fell off of them and hurt my ankle.

Other things, too, not as violent as the shoes but imbued with similarly tainted memories:

My grandmother's dark pink silk kimono embroidered with giant peonies and blue birds. I hung it on the back of the door of my room in the Berkeley hills where I was living when my father died. It's stained with mildew. My form-fitting, sleeveless wedding dress embellished over every inch with pearls like a mermaid bride's. A gold, reversible—lamé to lace—coat torn to shreds and my aunt's evening gown of mesh lace embroidered with gold, silver, and bronze sequin blossoms that I wore to punk clubs as a teenager and again on Halloween, as the fairy queen with a wreath of roses in my hair and my arms around a two-year-old Thomas the Train and a four-year-old Princess Jasmine before I left their father a few months later. My grandmother's 1920s wedding dress of yellowing satin rosettes and shredded lace that I wore in that author photo, later the subject of the scathing "review." My mother's wedding dress of gold damask that she'd worn when she married my father in a civil service. White was not for them. I'd worn the dress to win that 1950s dance contest with the sweet punk boy I'd stupidly rejected for the coke-head surfer.

All this needed to go. *I'll write about them*, I told myself.

My Secret moved the racks so the shelves stacked evenly. I hadn't realized how this symmetry could calm the brain.

I could even walk inside my closet now.

At night I don't have to sleep with the door shut tight; no demons threaten to emerge and suffocate me in the dark. If they appear in my dreams, I write them down, demon by demon, word by word, in my journal when I wake.

THE FOURTH DAY, we attacked the bathroom and the kitchen. These felt easier emotionally but more physically exhausting. We filled trashcans with junk stored under the sink; some was there when I moved in. We recycled old perfume bottles shaped like fans and doves and roses. We gave away small china boxes with flowers on top and crystal egg-shaped boxes and my mother's jewelry.

When she died I had a yard sale and sold all her antique cameos to one vulturous dealer for almost nothing. He came back to knock on my door for months afterward asking if I had more, but I pretended I wasn't home and didn't answer, not wanting to face either his disappointment or my regret.

In the kitchen lived my china botanical wedding plates and my mother's Delft plates and my grandmother's plates with the peacocks and gold trim, her English bone china floral teacups that I used to play with as a child, fascinated by the different varieties and specificity of the flowers—pink rosebuds, purple irises, yellow daffodils, white forget-me-nots.

There were my mother's wine glasses (including the rose and gold filigree ones that used to hold candles but might have lead in the paint) and pots and pans.

After relinquishing the books, the clothing, and the mementos, this seemed easy. Much of it just trash. Stained dishrags, torn potholders, pans with missing lids, expired vitamin bottles. Why did I keep them? Because I was afraid to spend money? Because I was afraid to let go of even the last shoddy traces of my dead mother, in spite of the fact that her face hovered around my living room, her clothes filled my closet?

I wanted to hold on to baskets full of doll-sized china tea sets, until My Secret showed me the bugs that had nested inside. I rescued, and disinfected, only a few of my grandmother's teacups to put on the top shelf of my cabinet with some plates and glasses that my children and I use.

I also kept the tall glass vases I'd collected from flower deliveries over the years. My Secret put them in the garage after I explained to him why I wanted them: "Someday we'll have a party," I said. "We'll put white votive candles from the 99 cents store and white sheets on the tables and fill the vases with peonies and lilies that we buy at dawn from the flower mart downtown."

"Okay," he said. "As long as you get rid of those tea sets with the bugs."

"I feel vulnerable. Having you see all my crap. All the dirt," I'll tell him later.

"I understand. It's okay. It's the same thing as me not having anything."

THE LAST TASK, on the last day, I did without him. Attachment theory. I'd learned, internalized what he taught.

It's okay to throw things in the trash.

It's okay to give away things to which I feel attached.

I'll feel better afterward.

I'll also feel regret. Regret is natural.

Instead, Esmeralda came over to help. Esmeralda, the only one who knew how to get me through the vitrectomy.

I asked her to help me get rid of almost everything in the garage. Her eyes signaled concern and she hesitated as I started to haul boxes and boxes into the dumpster I'd rented at My Secret's suggestion.

But after an hour or so, Esmeralda and I were tossing things over the rim of the dumpster: boxes of cards, letters, gift bags, old art supplies, collages, sketchbooks, college notebooks, term papers, original manuscripts, and, finally, every journal I'd ever filled.

When my mother died, she didn't only leave books and jewelry and china and cooking utensils and the dark wooden furniture I hated. She left boxes of pearl buttons and antique lace and reproductions of paintings by old masters, even old pieces of pastel-colored lint from the dryer. All of these for the collages she never made. (The lint, at least, was easy to throw away.) My brother and I then found the nude photographs and paintings of our mother, made by various boyfriends.

{ I don't want anyone to know what I felt. How I loathed my face and body. How I worshipped men I didn't know. It's all in my novels anyway. }

I don't want to leave my children with anything that can add more chaos to their lives, anything that can cause them pain. My published books are going to be hard enough. Maybe

my kids just won't read them; they've never seemed to have
an interest. Years ago, my too-young daughter had tried to
read my first book. She came to the subtly written rape scene
and put the book down. "I'm not ready for this now," she said.
Self-protection. I'm glad she has that trait. I seem to lack it
myself, but perhaps that's changing.

I don't want anyone to have to go through my journals.
I don't want anyone to know what I felt. How I loathed my
face and body. How I worshipped men I didn't know. It's all in
my novels anyway. But at least there I've distilled and shaped
pain into words and images that, perhaps, have some beauty,
that make some kind of sense.

What about the finished work? Is art just an expression
of egotism; are artists just elevated narcissists? What makes
someone's leftovers any more valuable than someone else's?
After we go, why should any part of us remain, except as a
memory in our loved ones' minds?

MY BROTHER STILL pays for a storage unit full of my dad's
drawings of nude women, paintings of his wife, sketchbooks
full of fragments of a life. How can we discard the art of a great
man? Even if no collector wants to buy the paintings anymore?

"We should have a pop-up store," My Secret said. "You can
sell some of your dad's art at good prices and then give away
what doesn't sell."

Even after this drastic spring-cleaning, my dad's paintings still festoon the walls of my house. I'm not able to part
with them yet. At the foot of my bed is his largest canvas—

it almost covers the whole wall. A vibrant blue background where flowers float.

My Secret Man looked at it from where we lay, legs and hands entwined in the bed one night, and said, "That flower in the center with the empty vase beside it is your mother, the white one floating horizontally above is your dad. The two white pansies abandoned to the side are you and your brother."

Abandoned to the side.

My father once told me, confiding as if I were one of the cronies he went to draw nude models with every week, "I've been told it's as if I paint with my penis."

I remember feeling queasy and shocked but I didn't know how to tell him it wasn't okay to speak to his teenage daughter this way. He'd also designed a cover for a book of my poems with a line drawing of a man and woman in coitus. "Is this all right with you?" he'd asked, showing it to me.

"It's beautiful," I said. The truth of the response didn't discount my discomfort.

When I told My Secret, he said: "I don't mean to pick on your parents, lover, but this part isn't normal. Just so you know. It wasn't your fault. It wasn't about you."

I want you to remember this, too: It might hurt but it's usually not about you. It almost never is.

ESMERALDA AND I put a piano, a television, a cabinet, and a bedframe into the alley. We threw a broken doll crib and a wrecked chair and more boxes and the tattered needle-point bench I'd once cried beneath into the dumpster. Giddy now, laughing so much our muscles liquefied and we had to pause, doubled over, sweating, covered with dust.

"That's my Francesca," Esmeralda said.

I was done worshipping at the shrine of pain.

At My Secret's request I sent photos of what Esmeralda and I completed.

"That's crazy. Do you realize what you've done? How much you've gotten rid of? Five porches-full, a dumpster and a half, six trashcans, two cars-full. Congratulations, lover. You did it."

I could not have done it without help.

My anxiety, whether genetic or environmental, makes it hard for me to organize space. But I can organize words, and teach others to do the same. Even during the most stressful times of my life, as my world shook or burned and my home and body teemed with anxious ghosts, I always wrote. The writing, even in its rawest form, helped me organize the chaos of my life.

Maybe this, too, goes back to my father instilling confidence in my artistic abilities but not in my physical body, which is after all, our first, final, and most significant environment.

One night, when we got back from dinner, Secret Man went into the garage, chose three of the thick glass vases we'd saved for parties and put one on my desk, in exactly the right spot, one on the mantel, and one on the white wooden storage unit next to the Tibetan box and a Tiffany lamp. We then filled them with pink peonies, pink and white roses, and white stargazer lilies with pink-velvet-leopard-spotted centers.

"To look at while you write," he said.

I THINK MY writing has improved in some ways since this purge. Even the students who come to my living room to write seem to have developed more quickly, as if the calm and order in the room focuses all of us. But the real organization is in the mind.

Why does this work?

On National Public Radio I heard a report about how MDMA, the substance known by ravers and club-goers as Ecstasy, can help people suffering with posttraumatic stress disorder. MDMA releases large amounts of serotonin, dopamine, and oxytocin that calm the patient to more readily be able to explore deep areas of trauma with a therapist. The drug has also been shown to decrease activity in the amygdala, the brain area associated with fear, and increase activity in the prefrontal cortex, where cognitive thought takes place.

> The outpouring and arranging words on a page has healed and comforted me.

From an early age, I've associated my own writing with expression, exploration, recognition, connection, acceptance, success, sustenance, and order. I can't obsess on the imperfections of my body, can't be afraid or anxious when my mind is too occupied with organizing chaos into something meaningful that might touch others, even heal and comfort them in some way. Just as the outpouring and arranging words on a page has healed and comforted me.

THE 12 QUESTIONS: SETTING
Question #7: What is the best setting for your book?

SETTING SHOULD BE more than just the background of your story.

Setting should reflect character. Each person will notice different details of setting. One way to choose what aspects of setting to describe is to think about **how the character is seeing the world.** Is she more concerned with nature or with the man-made aspects of her environment? Does he look down at the sidewalk and notice crushed petals and leaves diamonded with dew or does he always look up at the sky and out at the pink smog horizon? Everyone entering the same classroom will pay attention to different details: the faces of the people in the space, the clothing they wear, the lighting, the colors, the way the furniture is arranged. My characters, for example, are usually obsessed with facial features and expressions, clothing and flowers (surprise, surprise!).

Setting can be a character in its own right. The setting can have a **gift/flaw** and perhaps a **want/need.** The setting of a book can have an **arc.** A writer should know the depth and personality of the setting just as well as he knows his other characters.

Setting should move the story forward and provide conflict in the book. Obviously, the more threatening the setting, the more conflict it will provide.

SHANGRI L.A.

My ongoing effort to balance dark and light, pain and beauty, is expressed through the contrasts between the dangers and enchantments of Los Angeles, and I often use my city as a setting to add tension in my books.

Where I grew up in suburbia, danger lurked unnamed. At a sleepover at one friend's house, the girls and I snuck into the large, sterile kitchen. A handwritten sign on the refrigerator warned of weight gain, though the girl who lived there had bones protruding all over her body. I felt a chill of fear, like the frigid air on my skin, and couldn't sleep all night.

Years later I learned that the girl's father had installed hidden cameras to watch her and her friends undress.

At another friend's home, the dark, dank rooms threatened to swallow me alive. My friend's younger siblings ran around naked, scrawny and pale. Their father sat in a chair wearing sunglasses, long, stringy hair covering his face, watching them. He terrified me, but I had no words to explain this to my parents or even my other friends.

The friend who lived there ran away from home at sixteen and hitchhiked across the country.

When a mutual friend cautioned her of the perils of this, she simply laughed hoarsely and smashed out her cigarette. "That's nothing," she said, wrinkling up her freckled nose and shrugging her shoulders, then began to strum her guitar and sing.

To me, these stories are synonymous with a particular place and time: Los Angeles's San Fernando Valley in the 1970s.

People often tell me that Los Angeles feels like a character in my books. If my LA were a character:

> Her **gift** would be her seductive and glamorous allure.
>
> Her **flaw** would be her ability to disappoint and manipulate.
>
> Her **want** would be fame.
>
> Her **need**—which she has increasingly cultivated in the half-century-long **arc** since I've lived here—is depth.

However, even a peaceful, bucolic setting can provide a kind of tension if the protagonist is struggling with an internal conflict that won't allow her to experience the positive aspects of her surroundings, or if the contrast between the inner and outer worlds can be used to create deeper conflict.

Remember that no matter how evocative your descriptions (of setting or anything else), they shouldn't be there for their own sake. They should add what Donald Maas calls *microtensions* that move the story forward in some way, or add complexity to characters.

Here is how our sample authors use setting **to develop or reflect character, create conflict, or express theme**:

In *To Kill a Mockingbird*, small-town prejudice is the backdrop against which the story about the dangers of bigotry comes to life. Scout's initial flaw of close-mindedness is expressed through the culture of Maycomb.

In *The Great Gatsby*, the contrasting settings of the old-school West Egg and the more fashionable East Egg provide tension among Gatsby, Nick, Daisy, and Tom. The industrial dumping ground where Tom's mistress, Myrtle, is killed by Daisy is "a valley of ashes."

In *Jane Eyre*, Gateshead, Lowood, and Thornfield Hall provide three different settings and three specific sets of problems for the protagonist.

In *Wuthering Heights*, the dark, isolated, possibly haunted moorland farmhouse is symbolic of the entire story problem of the book. The house is a setting, and it is also a character.

Lolita's settings—first of claustrophobic suburban life and then of an almost surreal cross-country excursion—provide scenic conflict for Humbert and Lolita.

Play It As It Lays is set in Los Angeles in the 1960s; the movie scene, the freeways, the desert all create the perfect setting for the story of a lost soul searching for meaning. In an interview about her work and life in the *Paris Review*, Didion says that she grew up in an environment filled with danger; this sense of threat permeates the landscape of her novel.

Setting gives a specific context to your story. The reader can apply the message of the story to his own world more easily if the world of the story feels real, plausible, and specific. Even if a story is set in the past, the story problem can be relatable to today's audience if enough parallels can be drawn. For the same reasons, a fantastic or speculative setting must have valid, accessible "rules" so that the reader can more fully imagine herself within that world.

Whatever setting you choose, give it the detail and vibrancy it needs to improve and deepen your story by helping to define characters, build tension, and convey theme.

BY DEVELOPING YOUR setting, you will be cultivating the inner and outer landscapes of your own life.

6

ROSES AND BONES
—— Develop Your Style

STYLE HAS ALWAYS BEEN IMPORTANT TO ME, BOTH PER-
sonally and in my writing.

"I can remember almost everything I ever wore from the
age of twelve on."

I told this to Mateus, the Brazilian man I'd been dating and added, "I remember what I wore on all our dates."
(White eyelet sundress and bronze wedges; white velvet
trousers and pink satin camisole; suede and shearling jacket,
white thin wale cords, pink suede boots; black silk slip
dress, black Prada platforms, pink rose quartz globe beads;
pink satin embroidered Tahari baby doll dress and Lucite
leopard Prada heels; peach silk velvet dress. I spilled red
wine on it and dyed it in a vat of more red wine with the
help of a young, carnivorous Black-Irish woman who flirted

with Mateus and served him pork chops while I looked on, a
vegan in my stained finery . . .)

He regarded me with eyes so big and dark I couldn't gauge
their depth, or shallowness. "Is there a name for that condition?" he asked.

My twelfth birthday: a baby-blue stretch-fabric hoodie,
dark blue Ditto's jeans, and Kork-Ease sandals. My parents
took my friends and me to the Great American Food and
Beverage Company on Santa Monica Boulevard and we ate
Cobb salads and the waiter sang Cat Stevens songs.

My elementary school graduation: a peach French cotton
T-shirt and wrap-around skirt. My square dance partner was
a sullen, sturdy boy with acne roses on his cheeks. I had a
crush on him but we never exchanged a word.

My sixteenth birthday: a floral chiffon blouson top and
matching skirt with lavender suede wedges. I danced to "Black
Dog" by Led Zeppelin, which played on my friend's jukebox,
and kissed a boy in a peach polyester shirt that stunk of Brut
cologne. His name was Disco Bob.

My first concert at the Whisky a Go Go: a turquoise blue
taffeta 1950s prom dress and the black steel-toed engineer
boots I would hold onto longer than anything else.

The "ska riot" my friends and I incited at a *Dance Craze*
screening at the Egyptian Theatre on Hollywood Boulevard
(we heard the first strains of music and rose from our seats
to dance. By the time the bewildered usher had arrived to
tell us to sit down, the entire audience was up and skank-
ing): black ski pants with stirrups, a cream wool camisole

covered in pearls and opalescent sequins, and pink pointed-toed Keds sneakers.

My high school graduation: a leopard-print shirt, black capri pants, and black pumps. My skin was burned and swollen from lying in the sun without sunscreen. My friends, Elodie, Sasha, and Berry, tanned perfectly.

My college graduation: a white linen suit I'd bought with the money I'd won from a creative writing contest at school. My father had just died and I should have been grief-stricken, but in the pictures that were taken, my arms around my shell-shocked mother, I look a bit relieved. School and cancer were over.

The party for my first book: a patchwork miniskirt made of antique silk kimonos and a sheer organza blouse appliqued with thick white lace flowers. Angel, the first boy I wanted to marry, kept introducing himself to everyone as my "friend." In the pictures from that day, my grieving mother looks at least my age, if not a few years younger.

The party in Joshua Tree for the release of my fourth book: a vintage white satin dress with Doc Marten boots and a large hat swathed in white chiffon and roses. My hair was to my waist, a twist of dark extensions. Afterward my boyfriend Smoke and I made love in Casa Rosa, our adobe cottage on Harmz Way, and I frightened him with my screams.

My first date with my ex-husband: a pale blue T-shirt, white jeans, and pale blue patent leather Converse All-Stars. We discovered that we'd picked out the same names for the children we hoped to have one day.

The date when my husband and I got back together after our first big fight: a sheer, cut velvet minidress and silver Anna Sui sandals with snakeskin hearts on them. I believed that the shoes alone could make everything all right.

My wedding (of course): a mermaid dress covered in pearls. Now stained with rust.

My last trip to New York: a black bandage dress, black boots, and a thin, black, three-time-hand-me-down leather jacket that molded exactly to my odd dimensions. After a fight with my boyfriend at the time, I lost the jacket in a cab and tried to replace it with another, but that one was heavy, thick as hide, and never kept me as warm as the words I wrote to comfort myself when I got home.

MANY OF MY style choices came from women I admired: Patti Smith on the cover of *Horses* wore that white button-down shirt and black skinny tie to androgynous perfection, shattering and reshaping my ideas about what it meant to be a desirable, and powerful, woman artist.

Exene Cervenka taught me about the bewitching powers of vintage dresses, black stockings, and tiaras.

The iconic image of black-banged Chrissy Hynde in the red motorcycle jacket and red lace gloves seared itself onto my brain, and sent me on a lifelong search for the perfect punk chic look (and jacket).

STYLE ICONS

Substance is essential, but style counts, too. Both are necessary components of all forms of quality art: film, photography, painting, music. To develop your book's style in specific, concrete ways, try these exercises:

1. Imagine a fantasy *movie version* of your book: What would the scenery look like? Who would play your main characters?

2. Use Pinterest to create *inspiration boards* for your characters.

3. Use Instagram to discover *art and photography* that evoke the mood of your setting.

4. Use Spotify to make *playlists of songs* that your characters listen to, or music that creates a sense of place.

5. Use Polyvore to create *collages of your characters' clothing*.

Imagine what your favorite classic writers would have come up with if they had these tools available. What would Shirley Jackson put on her Pinterest board? What music would Faulkner listen to? What photos would Hemingway post on Instagram?

Jane Wiedlin of the Go-Go's with her pixie cut and red plaid kilt showed me the image of who I wished to be (if only I had pixie features to match, and could have played the bass).

Later, it was PJ Harvey, spidery in a hot-pink catsuit or wearing the shortest skirt and highest boots in front of a stadium of fans; her face remained placid while her hand strummed her guitar with orgasmic energy.

Although I bleached my hair blond at one time, the platinum beauty of Marilyn Monroe and Blondie's Debbie Harry always evaded me, but their personas were partially responsible for my alter ego's dandelion thistle hair. (1970s Cher was darker and had a big nose, but I didn't have her tan skin or height; with her long, natural, black mane and sheer, strategically beaded gowns she became the prototype for my alter ego's nemesis.) It was the smaller, paler, dark-haired, sometimes partially androgynous idols who helped me better see and value myself and strengthen the image I wanted to convey. Interestingly, they were singers and musicians rather than writers (although literary style icons Joan Didion and Donna Tartt couldn't look better). I guess I secretly wanted to be a rock star.

> What really matters is love and art. And just being alive.

When I had my daughter I forgot myself and just remembered what she wore: the white dress, with the elastic at the bottom and the tiny man in the moon on the front, to come home from the hospital; the white chenille dress with pink roses that she used to sweep the floor as she crawled around on her first birthday; the purple velvet overalls with silver flowers that she wore when she came to the hospital to have her adored-first-child heart broken by her newborn brother; the pale blue leotard embellished with jewels to become the Sugar Plum Fairy at the age of three. Though no one had told her to do so, she walked on the very tips of her toes through the entire performance. She'd seen the ballet after all and knew that's how these things were done.

YES, WHAT REALLY matters is love and art. And just being alive, no matter what you're wearing. I don't recommend cultivating the ability to remember everything you, or even your beloved child, have ever worn (especially when some of the memories, in my case, involved 1980s oversized shoulder pads and plastic neon pop-it beads). But it's fun to dress up. And it can be important, as a painter, rock star, or writer, to present oneself to the world in a certain way. Think about Frida Kahlo's self-portraits: her embroidered traditional Mexican dresses, pre-Columbian jewelry, cat eye glasses, hot-pink boots, and the flowers and ribbons that festooned her braids. All of this beauty hid and seemed to transform a body that had suffered and survived so much agony. For Frida, her style was her art and her art was her style. And both used beauty to combat pain and even death.

David Bowie played with style even more extravagantly, changing his identity at every turn: Davy Jones with his bangs and mod suit. Ziggy Stardust's blue eye shadow and shock of red hair. Aladdin Sane with that pink and blue thunderbolt, liquid color pooling in his clavicles—symbol of bifurcated freaks everywhere. The soullessly romantic Thin White Duke in a shirt white as his skin, cuffed to show his vulnerable wrists, open at the collar to reveal his vampire neck. Mime-face Bowie in a Pierrot costume embellished with tulle and metallic petals, topped by a white clown hat. Berlin Bowie, backlit, cynical-lipped and languid in an unzipped leather jacket, his hair the pale gold of certain roses, as he sings "Heroes" for the video.

Platinum pompadour Bowie in an oversized pastel pink suit for the *Serious Moonlight* tour.

Tin Machine Bowie, shirtless and sinewy at fifty in yellow and black striped bee pants.

Reality Bowie wearing a red, blue, and white Union Jack coat by Alexander McQueen—the back is scarred with cigarette burns, an eerie foreshadowing of what was to come.

Married Bowie smiling without artifice in a crisped white Dior Homme suit and shirt, photographed by Mario Testino for *V* magazine. Bowie in a white shirt with full sleeves, gold hair bright and straight, new white teeth almost as perfect as his wife's: he and Iman beam at their baby girl. Bowie with pre-Raphaelite hair, a pale blue striped extra-long shirt and a blue and creamy yellow floral brocade McQueen jacket. Bowie in a Deth Killers of Bushwick distressed tailcoat, black jeans, and Converse-style trainers on the 2004 tour that almost killed him. Bowie taming wolves in a shoot for GQ magazine: silver-gray cotton coat and pants splattered with black paint, black ruched jeans, a black cape, like a prince from an Eastern European fairy tale. Bowie in a red sharkskin suit, the color and sheen of blood, for his final live performance. Bowie in a black tuxedo with Iman, both effortlessly elegant and even more effortlessly enraptured with each other.

2016: David Bowie in a black Thom Browne suit and fedora, laughing in the face of Death.

If you think about it, in some ways, every fashion choice Bowie and Frida made were *fuck yous* to the Grim (and poorly dressed, I'm sure!) Reaper.

BECAUSE OF MY emotional attachment to my clothes, I'd struggled to clean out my closets with My Secret Man during our purge. And—for more than one reason—it was perhaps even harder to sell the pieces that seemed too valuable to simply give away.

"I have a lot of memories associated with this street," I told him when we went to Melrose with the trash bags full of clothing stacked in the back of my car.

Melrose in the early 1980s wasn't the cheap, throwaway trendy clothing or pricey designer places it would later become, but a wonderland of the punk, new wave, rockabilly, and vintage fashion and music, and avant garde art that inspired my early writing as much as any book I'd ever read. My friends Elodie, Sasha, and Berry and I pieced together ensembles with those brand new, never-been-worn, fresh-from-the-1960s canvas pointed-toed Keds from Cowboys and Poodles; two-toned suede and leather creepers with thick crepe soles, and leather jackets with pink and white diamond inserts from Let It Rock; ripped Levi's 501s, vintage prom dresses, shark-skin suits, or tattered sparkling tutus from Aardvark's or Flip. Dirk purchased bondage pants, combat boots, and kilts from Poseur. We went to street art openings at La Luz de Jesus gallery and bought strange wind-up trinkets, with chattering teeth and rollicking eyeballs, at Wacko.

Over the years we saw David Byrne, Cher, Thomas Dolby, Eric Stoltz, Jennifer Jason Leigh, Daryl Hannah, Stephanie Seymour, Bono's wife, and a gracious, petite, soft-spoken Iggy Pop shopping along that street. We spotted Angelyne, the life-size blond blow-up doll with heart-shaped sunglasses, cruise past in her hot pink Corvette, brushing her hair with a pink plastic doll brush. We watched the skinny, witchy Lava Lady (so named for the house she'd decorated in black volcanic rock), her hair sculpted into a point on top of her head, float by in her flared polyester pant suits and her six-inch platforms, as if she were walking the runways of her youth, pausing to peek into shop windows with shielded eyes.

Melrose was also where I once wandered alone and hungover, in a tight pink wife-beater. A man with a thick European accent followed me for blocks, badgering me to come home with him. I was fucked up enough that I considered it; did this mean I was beautiful? He reassured me, though, it did not. He just liked my tits in my T-shirt. The reason I didn't go with the man was less self-preservation than fanaticism. I pictured my obsession Smoke's eyes like topaz talismans as I walked to my car in the blinding, granular light.

> Melrose in the early
> 1980s was a wonderland
> of the punk, new wave,
> rockabilly, vintage fash-
> ion and music, and avant
> garde art that inspired
> my early writing as much
> as any book I'd ever read.

My friend Elodie briefly dated a hair stylist–to–the–punk rock–stars, with a Liberty spike Mohawk, a heavy German accent, and a salon on the deep east end of the street. While I waited for him to buzz Dirk's bleached flattop, I was so shocked to see a very petite and scruffy Prince that somehow I managed to poke myself in the eye with a long jagged fingernail.

I saw a man hit by a car on that street. The sound of his body on the concrete still smacks the air out of my chest when I remember.

This was near the Melrose funeral home where my once Marilyn-radiant mother's cancer-corroded body would be cremated thirty-five years later.

"You okay, lover?" My Secret asked me now.

"Yes," I told him. Now, holding his hand. But the street still swarmed with ghosts. Could I leave them behind with the clothes I hoped to sell?

First we went to Wasteland. He warned me they might be a little tough.

"Don't take it personally if they don't want stuff," he said.

How does he know me so well?

The blond Asian woman sorted through my clothes and plucked, with taloned nails, the multicolored sheer silk Pucci pants, the Lucite leopard Prada platform shoes that destroyed my feet, and the pastel designer T-shirts with my signature on the label from my collaboration with designer Kimberly Gordon. To my relief the clerk didn't turn up her nose at anything and folded each discarded piece carefully before she handed it back, then issued a check.

"How was that?" My Secret asked. "You okay?"

I nodded.

The ghosts of lost loves, would-be rapists, dead men and mothers, and unwittingly self-mutilating girls faded back into the past, unable to touch me, at least for now.

AT JET RAG on La Brea I sold a pale yellow hand-embroidered linen jacket made of handkerchiefs, the tiny Levi's denim jacket, the sheer silk organza blouse from my book party in 1989, and a hot-pink Ramones T-shirt. The women at the counter also took a stack of my bohemian, cut velvet scarves in a rainbow of colors—from my trance dance days with Jaedon.

I should have burned the scarves long ago.

AS IF TO change the subject, away from pain, Secret showed the buyers the black steel-toed engineer boots I'd bought when I was sixteen. The boots, along with the purchase of a pack of men's undershirts and two 1950s taffeta prom dresses, marked my transition into a punk rocker. No pain had ever infused the boots; I just wanted to move on.

"She's a writer," he told the women. "She's written a lot about the punk scene in Los Angeles in the early eighties. She wore these boots when she became a punk."

"Wait, you have to meet Orchid Satellite," one of the women said, summoning a girl with cartoonish glasses, bleached hair, and a baby-blue sweatshirt. Orchid hadn't read my books, and the women didn't buy the boots, but we seemed to have made some new friends. They wanted to know more about my writing, and I said, "He's a writer, too. He just doesn't like to talk about it."

"Is she your mentor?" one of the women asked him.

"She's my muse," he said. And something inside me cracked open with relief, like a favorite book, or the beginning bars of a favorite song that the pulse recognizes before the mind. Maybe I could be someone's muse after all.

I put my arms around his waist and his heart beat faster, I heard his breath quicken. "He's my muse and my mentor," I told the women at the store.

AT SQUARESVILLE ON Vermont, where the clothes have been curated in blocks of saturated vintage color, the bronze-skinned, bronze-curled clerk with breasts peeking out of her halter dress, and the tattooed blond in pigtails, a white off-the-shoulder peasant crop top, and white overalls, chose antique peach silk baby shirts, a thick cotton lace blouse, a pink beaded top, the Christian Louboutin pink satin sandals. They also took my mother's wedding dress.

Guilt circled my neck like the tattooed girl's choker as I watched her fasten a price tag to the dress. What statement was I making by sending it away? I'd disassembled the shrine. Had I committed sacrilege?

"More room for new things," My Secret said, sensing my concern. "More room to sit and write."

After he and I sold the clothes, we got smoothies at The Punchbowl next door. His, cacao and coconut; mine was the color of strawberries and tasted of roses. It's called a Rita Hayworth. I didn't lose any life that day. This was how life tasted. This was the taste of life.

OUR LAST STOP: Lux De Ville on Sunset in Silver Lake, a store crowded with vintage finery—denim, satin, brocade, velvet, rhinestones, lace. I've heard that Siouxsie Sioux shopped here. Three see-through dresses, designed by a Los Angeles ballet troupe leader, hung from the ceiling. A man with a beard and sad, dark eyes stood behind the counter. Almost closing time and he had somewhere to be but he generously let us show him what we had.

One of the first things he took from my bag was a yellow silk vest with hand-painted watercolor flowers. He recognized it from Aphrodite's store, the only item I'd saved. I'd given away all the other jackets and skirts made from the antique silk kimonos she'd repurposed.

"I used to shop there," he said. "Back in the day."

I told him I'd worked there. We instantly became part of the same tribe.

"It's a little stained," he said, stroking the silk vest with a fabric whisperer's hands, "so I can't buy it. But you should keep it. Wear it with what you have on now." Jeans. A black tank top. Suede wedges.

He chose, from the rest, a white denim Helmut Lang jacket, too small for me; a pink leather jacket, also too small; a silver chain metal belt; an antique wool and metal Art Deco purse that belonged to my grandmother; her cream moire silk strapless evening gown and matching ruffled coat; and some of my mother's jewelry. The silver and turquoise necklace from Mexico embellished with doves in flight, the stands of amber beads, the blue ring with the ivory cameo, the Art Deco pearl ring, the Victorian mourning pin made of glass and the woven hair of the dead. With the broken pink crystal beads the proprietor will make a necklace. (The glass cabinet is full of his own designs, including a silver cuff studded with jeweled insects.)

> A psychic on the Santa Monica pier once scowled at me darkly from beneath her heavy brows and warned, "There's a big project of yours. It's your life's work. But it will never happen until you give up believing that it will."

He gently clasped, with its scarab fastener, a child-size bracelet of green beads around my wrist.

"Keep this, it fits."

The last thing I showed him was my pearl-covered, floor-length, side-slit wedding dress. So heavy and sleek in my hands, it tried to slip away, like a mermaid, or at least a giant fish. When I wore it at my wedding I think I imagined all those pearls as ovulating eggs. My husband and I had been trying to get pregnant; we'd had one miscarriage already; another was to come.

"I don't think the rust stain will come out," the man said. "But you should keep this, too. Dye it pink. I can do that for you."

WHEN WE GOT to the car, My Secret looked a little pensive in the evening light, as the sun dropped lower against the bougainvillea and palm trees on the hills of Silver Lake. "I think you should show your engineer boots to him."

"I don't want to keep him," I said. "He has somewhere to be."

"Just try."

"These are from my punk rock days," I said when we went back in. "I wrote a few books about that time of my life in LA."

The man took the boots in his hands, assessing their size—they were unmarked. I think they must have been made for a boy or a very small man; women hadn't always been able to find this type of thing. I stomped through clubs in them—the Roxy, the Whisky a Go Go, The Vex, Cathay de Grande. I slammed in the pit below the stage. I dared boys to balance on my feet when all I really wanted was to stand on theirs.

Maybe the boots will be used in a movie version of my book, if it's ever made, I've told myself for over a quarter century. Even though a psychic on the Santa Monica pier once scowled at me darkly from beneath her heavy brows and warned, "There's a big project of yours. It's your life's work. But it will never happen until you give up believing that it will." Easier said than done.

JUST AS I can't seem to give up on the movie dream, I've never been able to give those boots away. In some ways, they were the most concrete symbol I had of the world that inspired my first book.

"I'll take them," the store owner said. Not as simple an offer as it appeared. He was giving me more than he knew.

This man, relieving me of my past, reminds me of the genie in my book, the one who granted three wishes. The wishes didn't turn out the way my protagonist thought they would—they came with loss—but love came, too. Love comes because it can. Sometimes you just have to wait long enough. As the wise ones say, sometimes you just have to let go.

I thanked the man. We shook hands.

"She's writing a book," My Secret told him.

"You'll be in it," I said.

"I'm honored."

"It used to just be about David Bowie," My Secret said. We'd passed a jacket on the rack with a painting on the back. A man with high cheekbones, a delicately carved jaw, bright red hair, and a thunderbolt across his face.

"That was so sad. When he died. He was such an important part of my life. It made me realize, we're next," the genie said.

We all stood there in the corner store with the ghost dresses hanging around us.

I shivered them off; it was time to live. Lightened of loads from the past, I took my lover's hand.

"Let's go eat," I said. "I'm starving."

"Vegan Reuben sandwiches and coleslaw from Flore?"

"Yes."

AFTER I'D SOLD and given away most of the things in my closet, only a small wardrobe remained: black tank tops from Target; white button-down shirts; a few discounted silk blouses; skinny jeans in denim, black, white, and light rose; light pink faux leather pants; a vintage leopard coat; a black motorcycle jacket (still not as good as Chrissy's); a denim jacket; a black tuxedo jacket; two pastel tweed jackets; a silk evening jacket embroidered with peonies; two Herve Leger bandage cocktail dresses from a discount place on the Internet; underwear and socks; tiger-print and pink-and-white-striped pajama bottoms; all-black yoga clothes; my shoes—the cute ones that don't hurt my feet, including sneakers that match the rose gold belts and purses My Secret had hung neatly on hooks. The whole process reminded me a bit of how Weetzie's beloved clothes are stolen from the back of her T-bird, forcing her to confront herself.

This is my style now: simple, functional, romantic, LA wordsmith, with some echoes of my punk roots, though the engineer boots have been sold to a tattooed Silver Lake hairdresser named Pony Lee.

TWO IMPORTANT PEOPLE taught me a lot about following my heart, staying true to my vision, and presenting my professional writer-self the way I wanted to be seen. My first guide in this endeavor was Tori Amos, whom I was fortunate enough to interview for *Spin* magazine in 1992. Those were enchanted days when a novelist with no journalistic experience could travel overseas to meet one of her favorite performers. The editor, Craig Marks, called me up and asked me what musical artist I'd like to interview.

Tori Amos? Yes, sure, she's in England right now. Do you want to go see her there or do it in the States? Just write your experience of her, as a novelist, don't worry about being too journalistic.

My mom and I took a plane to London, where we stayed in a little hotel by Kensington Gardens where Peter Pan had once frolicked with the fairies. White Corinthian columns, gold trim, chandeliers, spiral stairs, windows overlooking roses and courtyards. We ordered poached eggs, berries, and oatmeal and napped in the damask blue beds. Later that evening I met Tori's manager in the lobby and he briefed me on the next few days. A car would take me to her manor house in the Surrey countryside, where I would shadow her as she mixed *Boys for Pele*.

She wore a mohair sweater, gray trousers, and mary janes. The full lips and pale skin, the light eyes and rose-colored hair. The utter sensuality of that face, even the nostrils. I, like so many women of my generation and the one after, had treasured, wept over, and practically suckled *Little Earthquakes* and *Into the Pink*. (For me, the song "Winter" on *Little Earthquakes* was the only thing that expressed my struggle with self-love and my feelings about my father after he'd died, and it even mentioned the white horses that symbolized him.) She spoke our language, she wailed out our pain, frustration, and desire. She was recovering from Lucifer at that time, her dark prince, the focus of *Pele*.

Tori and I strolled through the countryside, along those roads, under those willows, talking about love and art and myth. Pele, the violent volcano goddess inside of her. How we women have one, and if we don't acknowledge her she will force us to keep chasing demon men, princes of darkness to wreak our own havoc upon us. I dined with her and the band, on poached salmon, baguettes, mashed potatoes, and pudding, in her elegant yet cozy candlelit dining room. The guitarist I had a crush on wasn't among them. I'd met him before; he was a friend of my ex-boyfriend Smoke's, had purportedly developed an insane guitar technique during the year he spent alone in his room nursing a broken heart. Tori put him on the phone with me, but the conversation writhed awkwardly between us.

I wasn't there for boys! I reminded myself. I sat by while one of my favorite performers on the planet mixed her album. She had read my book *The Hanged Man* and wrote some background vocals based on the book into one of the songs.

It was more than "A Sorta Fairytale," my visit to see her, make no mistake. And she the Faerie Queene. Perhaps I overemphasized the fae though. That's what I gleaned from a biography I read. Did she feel portrayed through an association with something more shallow than what she was intending? *Pele* was full of rage and sexuality, not little sylphs. But who am I to worry about Tori; she didn't need me to define her. After the article came out, I went to her concert and saw her briefly backstage. I had imagined we would be friends, then, but she had to hold court. I was only an acolyte.

Still, the connection lived on for me. Tori Amos and I had (and wrote about) miscarriages the same year, gave birth to daughters the same year. And she had given me something else as we walked those willow-shrouded country roads—the advice to take charge of my career: "Don't let anyone tell you how things should be. Stay in control of everything—book cover, images of you." Later, she let me use lyrics from "Bells for Her" in my book about two best friends in Hollywood and didn't charge me the customary fee.

David Lynch's then-wife, producer Mary Sweeney, once invited me to their home above the Hollywood Bowl to discuss my collection of short stories. I'd lived briefly in that part of town when my brother Zack took me in to recover from my eating disorder. His adobe home with the wood floors and big windows overlooked a vista of gleaming city that made my teeth ache like the Donut Stop confections Dirk and I ate at midnight after making the rounds of the Hollywood club scene.

My friend Elodie also lived in these hills, in a home she'd bought with money she'd earned as a set photographer. One could take an elevator up the hillside to the house with the wisteria vine as thick as Elodie's small torso and the bedroom where she once felt a ghost sit on her mattress and brush her cheek with its hand. (Even ghosts fell in love with her.) I remember standing in her tree house living room wishing that I could buy a place, too, one haunted with ghosts that loved me but were not my own.

{ To develop your voice, read widely, write consistently, and live fully. }

David Lynch was recording Jocelyn Montgomery's rendition of music by the twelfth-century Benedictine abbess, composer, and mystic Hildegard von Bingen. He played the dirgelike vocals for me in a small private amphitheater, the lights dimmed to perfect effect. Afterward, we spoke about my writing and aspirations to see my books turned to films.

"Just make sure you stay in charge," he told me, his face somber beneath the signature shock of hair, but with that twinkle that I find often in the eyes of the wildly creative. He then went on to share how he let one of his projects slip away from him creatively and always regretted it. As a fan of *Eraserhead, Elephant Man, Blue Velvet, Wild at Heart, Lost Highway* and, later, *Mulholland Drive,* I savored every word the way Jocelyn Montgomery sang Hildegard's lyrics—as if they imparted great and cherished wisdom.

WHAT I LEARNED, in the end, from both Tori Amos and David Lynch, as well as from my father, was to follow my inner knowing as an artist. Which is, perhaps, the true definition of personal style.

THE 12 QUESTIONS: STYLE
Question #8: What style will you employ to tell your story?

IT'S NO WONDER that the word *glamour*, which relates to **style**, originates from the concept of casting a glamour or spell. Likewise, style is a kind of magic you invoke to make your reader continue reading.

It's also one of the most difficult aspects of writing for many people and can take years of hard work to hone. But don't give up! Once you have your voice, the rest is much easier.

Style includes many things, such as diction, syntax, rhythm (or prosody), tense, point of view, figurative language, and tone. All style elements combined add up to **voice**. Your best voice is the one that comes naturally to you, without affectation. Don't try to be someone else when you are writing; let your individuality shine through your voice.

LET'S CONSIDER A few aspects of style and voice as they relate to the other 12 Questions:

> What does your writing style say about your main **character**?
>
> Is your character's **gift/flaw** reflected in the style? For example, if your character is brave but careless, do you use a bold, fast-paced style? If your character is highly introspective but overly cautious, do you use more interior ruminations?
>
> Is the character's **want** represented by the style of the book? If you are having difficulty distinguishing voices in your book, either in dialogue or through the narration, try to think about what each character wants. This will often determine their choice of words, their syntax, and the rhythm of their sentences, as well as the story content. A character who wants love, for example, will probably have a different voice than a character who wants power.
>
> Does the style of your book shift to reflect the movement of the character **arc**?

We can also learn from the style considerations in our sample books:

> In *To Kill a Mockingbird*, Scout's spunky young voice engages readers, exhibiting a youthful humor mixed with a sophisticated lyricism; this balance defines the style of the book and the tension between the young

Scout in the story and the older narrator looking back on her life.

In *The Great Gatsby*, Fitzgerald uses the plainspoken Nick as a peripheral narrator to create a style in which Gatsby can be mythologized, making him appear more formidable than if the story were told through Gatsby's own dramatic voice.

Jane Eyre is filled with fairy-tale imagery. Practical Jane tells the reader that "a fairy" suggests she advertise in the paper for the job that brings her to Thornfield as a governess. On first seeing the mansion, she describes it as a "fairy place" and later as "Bluebeard's castle." Similarly, Rochester calls her "unearthly," "sprite," "changeling," and "witch," as well as "fairy." This style evolves with Jane: she uses less fairy imagery as the book progresses, as if she is outgrowing this more childlike and magical way of seeing the world, or at least integrating it into her life.

Wuthering Heights is told by two peripheral and subjective narrators who help us suspend our disbelief as we enter this strange, dark world. The wealthy young Mr. Lockwood's voice is more formal and staid than the servant Nelly Dean's, but both narratives reflect Bronte's gifts with language that evokes the darkness and the romanticism of Gothic literature.

In *Lolita*, Nabokov created an entire language to reflect Humbert's obsession.

Clipped, *clean*, and *spare* might be words to describe Didion's style in *Play It As It Lays*. The prose expresses

Maria's thin, elegant frame, and the fragmented storyline reflects her broken state of mind.

It's fine to write a full rough draft in a voice that doesn't
quite work, but if you develop your style early on, you'll find
a more authentic story. (For exercises to help you develop
your own signature style, see page 151.)

Creating an effective style might take time and work and
heightened awareness. **To develop your voice, read widely,
write consistently, and live fully. A strong writing voice can
connect us to others, and more deeply to ourselves.**

7

GUARDING THE MOON
—— Persevere

W HEN I BECAME PREGNANT FOR THE FIRST TIME, I
never imagined anything could go wrong.

My fiancé and I had conceived on one try after stopping
birth control the night he surprised me with his grandmother's
diamond engagement ring in an Altoids box and asked me to
marry him. Except for some mild, almost pleasant nausea,
the pregnancy was going well. At three months I was doing yoga; taking long walks with Vincent Van Go-Go Boots;
drinking carrot juice, banana, and vanilla yogurt smoothies;
writing a book; and enjoying my husband-to-be.

I immediately fell in love with the child in my womb.
I had somehow decided he was a son, and my fiancé and
I named him Samuel after both our maternal grandfathers,
both engineers and two of the sweetest men who had ever

lived. We knew our Sam would be just as sweet. I started a journal, telling him how ecstatic I was, how ready for his arrival. *I've been waiting my whole life.*

But when I went to the doctor for an ultrasound, no heartbeat blinked on the screen. There was no child. I drove home in shock and fell to the floor, where Vincent tried to lick the tears from my face. The next day, my fiancé took me to the doctor to have my womb emptied, and I bled heavily that night. The pain was a hollow, haunted thing.

No one had ever told me about experiences with miscarriage before but slowly the stories started to come. *At twelve weeks, at sixteen weeks, at birth. Stillborn. But we tried again.* Or: *We adopted. Look who we have!*

My second miscarriage was, perhaps, less traumatic for me, but more so for my then-husband. I hadn't bonded with this "baby" yet, hadn't communed with this soul or even named him, or her.

When the doctor showed us the penumbra in the ultrasound, no heartbeat sparked that darkness either. My husband wept for the first time then, standing there by the ultrasound machine; standing beside helpless, shivering me with my stirruped feet; covering his face with his hand, turning away from the uncomfortable silence in the room. I hadn't realized until that moment how our relationship might depend on this shared goal of a child.

But we did not give up. We went to a fertility specialist. We ran tests. We followed the advice of doctors, friends, magazine articles. And I got pregnant again.

I received acupuncture treatments and did gentle yoga and took slow walks in sunshine. I sat under the grape arbor in the backyard, beside the orange tree, eating the sweetest oranges I'd ever tasted—fertilized by our own Palms, California backyard soil—reading and dreaming of my child. Ladybugs crawled across my windshield and up and down my arms on a weekly basis. I took this as a very good sign; I'd never experienced such a blessed insect orgy.

For the first three months, I was too sick to eat much except those backyard oranges, but between three and five PM I craved, animalistically, vegetarian burritos, and my husband rushed out to bring them to me, insides fresh and steaming, almost melting the thin tortilla, clues to the appetite of the child who would come into our lives.

Nine months later, our soon-to-be-burrito-eating daughter, Jasmine Angelina, was ready to be born! I'd longed for her as much as for my son. I'd imagined having a daughter since I was a young child myself, caring for scores of female baby dolls with names like Leetie Doll, Tiny Tata, and the pink papier-mâché, glitter-painted beauty, Picnic Rose.

In a dim hospital room above the pellucid night city, R. Carlos Nakai's Native American flute music transported me as I paced around, waiting for the contractions to speed up. I hadn't wanted an epidural but the nurses insisted and I wasn't strong enough to say no. Nor was I strong enough to argue with the obstetrician who told me, "Hurry up, Francesca, push, I have a golf date with my son" (it was Easter

Sunday). I pushed. I screamed. I tore. He sewed me up unceremoniously. He left. The baby was placed on my chest. Nothing else mattered. My heart cracked open like a pomegranate, spilling shiny red bittersweet seeds, like blood that had been turned to light.

I wept when they took her away to wash her. I couldn't stand to be separated for a moment. They brought her back. I tried to get her to latch on. My mother helped. It hurt. It worked. The baby suckled. I wept some more.

She slept beside me in a little plastic box like my own Snow White. In the night I woke and turned and saw her dark blue eyes surveying me, a little alien in a night cap and onesie decorated with a sleeping moon.

I called my husband and woke him. "She's looking at me," I said. He chuckled and humored me while I sang her praises until he fell asleep on the other line. She was still up, looking, looking.

The episiotomy hurt much worse than the miscarriages, my head burned from the aftereffects of the anesthesia, and my nipples cracked and bled, but I'd never felt happier to be in my body. I loved my milk-leaking breasts and my strong loins and my tangled hair and sleepless eyes. How could I not love a body that had delivered this baby to the world and was now sustaining her?

FOR MY FIRST year as a mother, I had the luxury of being able to stay home with my child. Unable to collect enough stories about newborns to satisfy my thirst, we lay nursing on the futon while I watched a reality TV show that chronicled the birth stories of various families.

We went to the library and I read all the classic picture books aloud to my child. I put her in the stroller and roll-erbladed along Venice boardwalk. I took her to baby yoga, music class, and the park. I wrote my first nonfiction book, a memoir, about the only subject that interested me then: being a mother, *her* mother.

I was so in love that my husband and I decided to start trying again, although our doctor warned us against it. "Be happy with what you've got," he said. But we didn't listen, even though I would be thirty-nine and a half by the time this second child was born. If he or she was born. Could my body take another miss? Could my heart?

When we'd first been set up by friends, my husband and I had discussed our desire for children. Sitting at that café in the Valley (so near to where I'd grown up and so far from Ohio, the place he'd left for warmer climes), eating fruit-juice-sweetened pastries, we also discovered that we'd picked the same two names: Sam, as mentioned, for our maternal grandfathers, and Jasmine, because we loved the white, sharply sweet-smelling flower that filled the air of Los Angeles at night. We'd even picked the same alternate name for a girl: Jade.

Secretly, I did want a boy this time. And not just any boy. I wanted Sam, the one I'd lost. I believed that somehow his soul was still out there, waiting for a body to receive him.

Crazy as it sounded, part of me wondered if he'd chosen to wait, didn't want to be my firstborn. It was a big responsibility, to take on all my smothering mother-love, almost forty years in the making.

My daughter could handle it, and with aplomb. We interacted like passionate, if chaste, newlyweds, arguing, crying, then making up with a wild abandon of hugs and kisses. That first year there were always flowers everywhere. Bouquets of lilies and jasmine plants for the garden. There were baby dresses covered with cabbage roses, Chinese satin pajamas embroidered with peonies, and tiny leather shoes with daisies on the toes. I dressed myself in bright floral kimono prints. I wore jewel-studded clothing that refracted the light. For her delight.

Sam would have been overwhelmed. He was waiting, I told myself, for me to just calm down a little bit.

On 9/11 I went in for an ultrasound. The doctor, a new one (we'd dumped the golf-player), looked at me grimly.

"No heartbeat," he said.

On the way home I kept thinking, *A national disaster has occurred. The worst one ever. We are all in shock. Why should the doctor care? Why bring another baby into this world? My pregnancy doesn't matter.*

But I couldn't help it. It did matter. It did.

I called another doctor, one a friend had recommended. Paul Crane. His voice gentled me. It matched his placid, handsome face, though I hadn't seen him yet.

"It might be too early," Doctor Crane said. "Come see me in another week. And don't worry."

I'm not sure why I believed him; what reason did I have for hope? The world was falling down around us all, like those bodies jumping from those towers. When I'd witnessed them on the TV screen, pressing my sleeping daughter's face to my chest so she wouldn't wake and see, I'd thought they were bits of debris, or ash. Or birds.

As I'd done my whole life, I'd used metaphor to protect myself, to protect the child in my arms, the one in my womb. If he was still there at all. And could anything protect us?

I went to see Doctor Crane. He squirted the cold jelly onto my belly. He moved the probe around. He found the fetus. He found the beating heart.

He found Sam. Sam was there.

Somehow my husband, my daughter, Sam, and I had persevered. Against all odds, in a cruel and broken world, where planes crashed into towers, where people leaped from crumbling buildings, in spite of all, we had made a family.

Sam's birth had its own strange tale, even after that. I'd asked Dr. Crane for a private labor coach, and he'd sent a woman my husband and I immediately liked. Before she left, I asked her if she'd be present at the birth as a doula.

"I'm sorry," she said. "I don't do that work anymore."

After she left, I called her. I didn't know why, but I knew I needed her there with me when Sam was born.

"I'm sorry," she said.

"Please," I begged. This wasn't like me. My husband shook his head in mild astonishment.

There was a pause.

"All right," the woman said, "I'll do it for you guys. I haven't done that work for a few years but I like you both."

Sam missed his due date and my husband and I went to visit the doula at her home. She showed me a picture, blown up on one wall, of a determined young man striding down a runway beside an indigenous woman. With his dark curls, high cheekbones, and prominent nose, he looked, oddly, like a combination of my husband and me, like a child we might have had.

"He's so handsome," I said.

"Isn't he?" said the doula. "He lives in Berkeley with his fiancée. He does humanitarian work in Colombia. And you know, his birthday is in a week."

"Maybe he and Sam will have the same birthday," I said.

A week later, on the eve of the doula's son's birthday, I went into labor. This time I didn't take drugs. Instead I stared into the doula's eyes and held her hands.

"You can do this," she said. Her face was fierce. I believed her. She'd seen something, something I couldn't quite understand. She knew what real pain was. Her eyes said: *Your pain? This isn't it.*

Doctor Crane came in with his hair standing up every which way, one shoelace untied—an absent-minded professor. Unlike the oblivious golfer, Crane told me not to scream, to save my energy. And, probably, to save his own finely tuned nerves. It wasn't easy to deliver this large boy but the doctor managed it, in the nick of time, without a C-section. Sam was placed on my chest. This time when the nurse tried to take him to be washed, I asked that she do it there in the room and she kindly obliged. When he was back in my arms, I turned to the doula.

"I'm sorry for keeping you from your son's birthday," I said. "What are you going to do to celebrate?" I don't know why I chose to mention it in those first moments after my baby's birth, why it felt so important to say.

The doula looked at me. There were dark rings around her eyes. They'd been there every time I'd seen her, as if she never slept well, but I hadn't really paid attention to them before. Grief, that was what I'd seen in her face, but I'd been too caught up in my pregnancy to know. She shook her head. "It's a sad story," she said. "I can't tell you right now. Right after you've given birth. This should be a happy time."

> To survive in this life—and maybe even to come back again like intrepid ghosts—we must persevere.

"Please," I begged. It seemed I was always begging her; I couldn't seem to help it. "Please, you have to, please, I want to know."

"My son was killed," she said. "He was murdered trying to help save the rain forests. I didn't want to tell you when you saw his picture. I didn't want to upset you while you were pregnant."

For the next few months I sat up at night nursing Sam, watching, over and over again, a video about the doula's son, the one who had my son's birthday, a video about the young man who had been killed execution-style for trying to help save the rain forests in Colombia.

He had never given up. My struggle seemed trite in comparison. And yet I was reminded that, as humans, perseverance is one of our greatest strengths. Sometimes it is all we have.

This young man continued to touch my life. A few years later, after I had divorced my husband and moved out with my kids, Jaedon, the strange yoga instructor I'd started to see, came over with a video he insisted we watch. It was about a guru Jaedon admired, and I found myself drifting off until a slender young woman with dark curls came onto the screen.

"He helped me so much after the death of my fiancé," the woman said.

I looked up. I knew right away. This was the fiancée the doula had spoken of. The young woman went on to recount the story of her beloved's brutal death and how she had eventually healed by letting him go, while still acknowledging their undying connection.

I felt as if the man had entered the room and touched me lightly on the shoulder. *I am here.* Maybe Jaedon had come into my life solely for this. It helped me reconcile that relationship later on.

WHEN I'D LEFT the hospital in a wheelchair, clinging to my newborn baby like the lost and found love he was, a nurse saw us and smiled. "Looks like you kind of like him," she said. "Do you think you'll keep him?"

I hadn't let go of him since his first conception. I wondered if I ever could.

When we arrived home, my distraught daughter ran out the front door and huddled on the front porch overgrown with the jasmine flowers we'd planted just after her birth. I knelt beside her and heard a crunch; she chewed on a plastic spoon, it had broken into small bits. Horrified, I made her spit it out and held her in my arms.

"I'm having a hard time, Mommy," she said, tears shining like dew drops on her rose petal cheeks. She was only two years old, but so articulate—she'd been speaking in twelve-word sentences since before she turned one—and suddenly she seemed big to me. Compared to the baby. It wasn't fair.

While I was pregnant with him, she'd contracted rotavirus, a disease now inoculated against; it's that virulent. She couldn't keep any food down, or even water, weighed under twenty pounds. The doctor had us check in to the hospital, and when the nurse had to put a needle in my daughter's thread-like veins to feed her, I hovered above, waiting to give her my breast. I held her in my arms all night, though the tubes in her arms and my pregnant belly made it hard for either of us to sleep. But we were together.

By morning she was better and we ate dry Cheerios and watched cartoons. A nurse gave her a doll. We went home and I dressed Jasmine in a pink velour onesie with ears, a tail, and the word *Fifi* scrawled across the front.

She'd put her hands on my expanding belly and wriggled with disgust: "The baby is icky." When we brought her a stuffed teddy bear and said it was a gift from him, she'd been skeptical: "How could he *buy* that?" Now he had fully infiltrated her life. All I could do was tell her how much I loved her, how she was my first, my girl, my one and only, the first real love of my life.

The baby Sam seemed hale and hardy and I thought some of my neurosis would calm now that he was here. Until he began to develop ear and sinus infections. We had to treat them with antibiotics that hurt his stomach. I stayed up all night walking with him in the misty air outside to help him breathe. Dark circles shaded his green eyes and his naturally tan skin turned pale. He grew more withdrawn and slept for hours instead of leapfrogging around on the floor to play with his beloved train sets or toddling through the house after his sister as he had done before.

I finally couldn't bear to give him any more of that sickly sweet medicine that messed with his digestion, and so I changed my diet, added probiotics, and took him to an osteopath who treated him weekly with body work that cleared the ear passages. He got better. Thank god.

Like any parent, I am utterly vulnerable to anything that might harm my children. I'd wanted them so much. They could so easily destroy me. They knew it, and every time they hurt themselves they looked to me with pleading eyes. I realized they weren't only seeking comfort and reassurance that they were okay; they wanted to know if I would be, too.

To survive in this life—and maybe even to come back again like those intrepid ghosts—we must persevere. This seems to get harder and harder as the world falls apart around us. But it also becomes clearer that we must not give up.

We must persevere like the young man who died saving rain forests, or even like my children, surviving the "everyday shocks" of homework, tests, sports, social challenges, sibling rivalry, the political climate, living in two homes, and a harried single mom.

As artists, we have similar challenges. We have to keep working, no matter what. We have to seek inspiration through muses and mentors and by exploring our pain, and when we don't find that inspiration, we have to keep creating anyway.

The former poet laureate of West Hollywood Steven Reigns originally studied with Natalie Goldberg, author of *Writing Down the Bones*.

"She's been encouraging people for over thirty years to write," Stephen says. "She's jokingly said her advice is simply to 'sit down, shut up, and write.'"

One of the greatest challenges of being a writer isn't just finding motivation; it's supporting yourself financially while you're creating art. Mary Pauline Lowry worked at the National Domestic Violence Hotline, "which allowed me to be of service and offer crucial help to women, even as I heard fascinating (and painful) stories that filled my creative well. . . . I think it's important to find a job that shelters your writing life . . . a job that pays enough to live on and doesn't use up all the energy and focus."

Of course, when you reach the point where you *are* supporting yourself as a writer, motivation can come more readily, but not always.

THE 12 QUESTIONS OF *BELOVED* BY TONI MORRISON:

Sethe **wants** to forget the past and **needs** to face and confront it in the form of the revenant, Beloved, who may be the ghost of Sethe's murdered daughter.

Sethe's **gift** is her strength and survival skills, but taken to an extreme, her **flaw** of excessive—though, considering the circumstances, understandable—force causes her to take her two-year-old daughter's life in order to "escape" the horrors of slavery.

Sethe's **arc** begins with trying to repress the past and moves to facing the past and then toward her finding love with Paul D. Her primary **antagonist** is Beloved.

The **setting**, a place and time of slavery and its aftermath, provides conflict and context for the plot.

The **crisis** emerges when Beloved begins to take over Sethe's life.

The **climax** occurs when Sethe kills the white man who has come to offer Sethe's daughter Denver a job.

The **resolution** is found when Beloved vanishes, Denver moves on with her life to become part of a larger community, and Paul D. returns to Sethe.

The **style** combines fragmented prose, perhaps to show the effects of slavery on the body and mind, with straightforward, lucid exposition. Morrison's poetic voice alternates between showing and telling.

The **theme** of *Beloved* is the need to face the past in order to create change in the world.

Julia Cameron, author of *The Artist's Way*, advises that all writers produce three "Morning Pages" of longhand, stream-of-consciousness work written upon waking. The key to this is consistency and, again, perseverance.

Another way to keep writing is to make a contract with yourself. Try listing the amount of pages you'll be writing each month and the books you'll be reading. Pick books that interest you and will help your writing in specific ways, and when you've finished reading one, write three paragraphs about the book—a summary, a single craft element, and how you will use that craft element in your own work.

The contract should be as specific and honest about your writing challenges and goals as possible. For example, instead of just saying: "I will write twenty pages a month and read and annotate two books," try to zoom in on craft elements that need improvement, like "I will work on creating more tension by developing my antagonist, making my protagonist more sympathetic by adding action, and find ways to improve my voice by avoiding clichés and showing rather than telling whenever possible." You can also then choose your books according to these goals.

On the first day of the year, I created a three-column document, one column for "gratitude," one for "accomplishments," and one for "goals." By starting with "gratitude," I not only countered any negative feelings, I could also see my priorities more clearly. The "accomplishments" column obviously emphasized what I'd done. After I'd written these two columns it was easier to see what matters to me, what was lacking, and where I could improve. In the same way, this system can work for writing.

What in your creative life are you grateful for? The emotional support of a partner, friend, colleague, or teacher? The time to write after work and on weekends? The local library? National Novel Writing Month (NaNoWriMo)?

What have you accomplished? A first draft of a chapter? A trip to a writing conference? Signing up for a writing class?

What are your goals? A second draft of your novel? More weekly hours devoted to your work? Submitting stories to journals?

And what fuels this gratitude, accomplishment, and goal seeking?

Perseverance.

By reminding ourselves of what we are grateful for, we feel fortified, no matter how challenging life becomes. Our accomplishments are the result of hard work. In the same way, our goals, when clearly stated through the lens of our gratitude and accomplishments, can feel less daunting, feel as if they can eventually be achieved, if only we persevere.

> Even if life is temporary, we have the chance to make the most of it through our stories.

NOT EVERYTHING IS within our control. I was both blessed and lucky to have given birth to two healthy children, as well as to have been able to publish books. But the work toward those goals was an essential, and ultimately fulfilling, part of the process.

Even if I never published my books, I would at least have had the experience of writing them.

Even if I never gave birth to my children, their souls would somehow have found me.

Even if life is temporary, we have the chance to persevere, to make the most of our existence through our stories.

THE 12 QUESTIONS: THEME
Question #9: What is the theme of your book?

THE THEME OF your book represents the underlying beliefs your book will impart to the reader through story. It's the deep message or core belief you are trying to get across to your reader without being didactic.

The theme is related to your character's **arc** and can be stated as a cause/effect sentence. For example:

In *To Kill a Mockingbird*, Scout changes from a closed-minded, naïve girl to a compassionate, mature one, and this arc determines the theme: We must open our hearts to treat others with kindness and morality as equals, and protect the innocent, in spite of the evil in the world.

Here are more examples:

The Great Gatsby: If we never let go of the past, we
   will suffer and ultimately be destroyed.
Jane Eyre: If we balance reason and passion, we will
   find true love, including self-love.
Wuthering Heights: If we are treated cruelly, we will
   treat others with cruelty.
Lolita: Obsession is both seductive and dangerous.
Play It As It Lays: In order to truly live, we must take
   risks and love acutely, meaningfully "play the game."

Look to see if themes are emerging in your work, and if so,
consider how you can heighten them. If you don't find themes,
how can you introduce an element that reveals a higher truth?

Turn to your own beliefs for guidance: What do you
believe is right and wrong? If you were to die tomorrow,
what viewpoints about life would you want to leave behind? Write your answers down. And don't worry if they
sound cliché—in fact, they probably will, as that is the nature of universal truths. But your writing will not be cliché;
it will offer a unique, personal expression of how you see
the world.

**Crafting a theme is like taking your heart out of your
chest and putting it on the paper in front of you. Which, if
you think about it, is why many of us write.**

8

BEYOND THE PALE MOTEL
—— Face Your Fears

F OR YEARS I BELIEVED MY MOTHER CAST NO SHADOW. She inspired and championed my work, read all my early drafts, and helped me out financially so I could spend time writing. She encouraged me to explore my psyche and didn't shy away from my books about incest, or rebuke me for writing less-than-flattering mothers. But when it came to violence, I knew my mother would balk. She had always lived—with great determination—in the light (like the medieval tin Madonna that hung on the wall of my Jewish childhood home, surrounded by roses and a nimbus crown). So, to appease my mother, to keep her comfortable, I unconsciously avoided writing anything *too* disturbing, too dark.

After her death I began to excavate these themes. They had always intrigued me. (Case in point: that fourth-grade play called *Help* about the doll with bleeding eyes; Mrs. Eisenmann kindly indulged me but, perhaps wisely, chose not to share this masterpiece with my parents.)

I'd written one short story that I'd wanted to develop into a novel. Based on the fairy tale "The Three Heads in the Well," my story told of a woman whose father wants to marry her after her mother dies, so she runs away from the motel he owns in the desert, to become a stripper in Hollywood. She meets a forensics photographer, and they are soon both involved in a murder case involving decapitation. The heads of the women that have been killed sing to the protagonist in warning. My mother shuddered when I even mentioned it, and though it was published as part of a short story collection, I never revisited it as a longer work.

But after my mother died I began to write a very dark psychological thriller. All I knew was that it would take place in Los Angeles and the main character, Catt, would be a hairdresser at a Silver Lake salon called Head Hunter; work out at a gym called Body Farm; that she'd have a best friend with a young son named Skylar whom Catt loved; that Catt's punk rock musician husband, Dash, would leave her; and that she would start sleeping with a lot of random men. I knew there would be a serial killer who severed and collected body parts of women to make a new, "perfect" woman. I had no idea who this character would be or why it felt so important to write the story.

Later I realized that the book was a metaphor for my own fraught experiences with both my body image (starting with my childhood crush telling me I'd be cute if someone cut off

my head; thus, the severed parts) and with Internet dating.
I also saw this project as a latent rebellion against my lumi-
nous mother whom I had tried to protect. (I always wanted
to cover her eyes when anything disturbing popped onto a
movie theater screen, and I cringed and lowered the sound
when someone screamed on TV, so she wouldn't hear from
the next room.)

The killer emerged full-blown in my mind when a screenwriter friend sat me down after reading the first rough draft
and pointed out that I'd written a murder mystery without
a murderer. But when I began to revise, I realized this character symbolized, more than anything, the self-destructive
impulses within myself.

I'd never really dated before my forties. I'd always just
met someone and fallen into a relationship with him, remaining alone for years in between. After the Brazilian, Mateus, came over to the pale yellow cottage I'd just bought,
sat me down in the fairy garden by the lily pond croaking
with frogs, under the big sheltering tree that would, though
I didn't know it yet, soon die and need felling, and told me
he didn't want to see me anymore, I cried so hard into my
knees that my pink and white tie-dyed yoga pants were forever stained with mascara.

At one point, I'm rather ashamed to say, I actually got
down on those very knees and drew the shape of a man in the
air, pleading to the universe to send me my beloved. It felt
as if my life would never be complete without him.

So I wiped away my tears, threw out the yoga pants, and
turned to the Internet with determination. I believed I was

finally strong enough to handle this kind of dating. I had my new home, my two children, my loving mom, good friends, my health, and my career. Just as I didn't know that the best thing in my garden—the old tree—would die, I had no idea that during my search for romantic love, almost everything on my gratitude list would soon be threatened or taken from me.

THINGS HAPPENED SO fast online. Who needed to spend hours in bars, worrying about kids at home with the babysitter? You could just click on a picture, and if things worked out you could arrange an efficient coffee date in twenty-four hours. In those first few weeks, this Luddite had found in technology a balm for my sorrows and frustrations.

But I soon became overwhelmed. There were so many different types of people and so much electronic energy coming at me! I needed a way to understand what was happening, some kind of taxonomy. For this I turned to mythology and fairy tales because those stories have always informed my life and my work. I believed this knowledge would empower me and, somehow, keep me safe in the real world, just as it had in the world of my imagination and writing. Soon, my potential dates began to sort themselves: aggressive Werewolves, laid back Mermen, moody Centaurs.

After some research and self-reflection, I classified myself as Wood Nymph—emotional, sexual, passionate, somewhat disheveled, and wild at heart. I began to create categories for all the people I knew.

Following a series of disappointing coffee dates with smart, sarcastic Hobgoblins and timid, pouting Giants, I had a conversation with an artist who sounded promising. He painted large encaustic paintings made with beeswax so they smelled like honey, he explained; he sounded articulate and funny on the phone, with a lovely, deep voice.

When we met, this man, Carlton, showed up dressed in a fawn-colored suede jacket, jeans, and Chukka boots. He seemed shy and skittish but friendly. We talked about art, books, movies, music, yoga, and meditation. A pleasant chemistry flickered between us in spite of his slightly off-putting stiffness.

He embodied how I imagined an elf (in the original Norse sense) would manifest in the modern world—lithe, spry, skittish, intelligent, a little cranky, and noncommittal. But he wasn't just any elf, I decided—he was a very specific kind of modern elf who loved technology, lived online as much as off, and, as a city dweller, had been removed from nature, the thing that originally sustained his soul. The *Urban* Elf.

I had noticed that this Urban Elf's online profile stated he was "separated," so I asked about this early on in the evening.

His eyes widened behind his small rectangular glasses and he sat up even straighter. "Yes," he said, rather defensively. "We're separated. She lives in Canada with her boyfriend."

I didn't inquire further. I could tell he didn't want me to, and I obliged him out of my own fear of facing the truth. I wanted this to work out because of the warm late summer night, because I was lonely and trying to forget Mateus. Anyway, she had a boyfriend.

Carlton and I talked in an animated way for the rest of the evening and then he walked me to my car, kissed me quickly, and darted off.

We went out on a few more dates after that. He invited me over to his very neat, tastefully furnished apartment and showed me his artwork. His skill was undeniable and the paintings did, truly, smell like honey. But, I noticed, the objects he depicted cast no shadows. I saw a small photo of a woman on his mantelpiece and once again, chose to disregard it. Carlton and I made out and though things got hot and heavy there was a certain reserve to his behavior. He avoided deep eye contact and kisses, and hurried me off as soon as the make out session ended.

After a few more dates I began to feel unsure about this man. I couldn't read what he was feeling. He seemed uncomfortable with the idea of my children and didn't want to go anywhere that involved other people, preferring to stay in his apartment most of the time. Our relationship fell away, though we continued to communicate occasionally by email.

But as I dated more incompatible men in the name of research, I began to miss Carlton. I realized that he and I had more in common than I had thought at first and, frankly, he inspired me as a fellow working artist. We exchanged some texts (he wasn't big on phone calls) and decided to meet.

We got together for a drink in the lobby of the Culver Hotel under the Art Deco milk glass, vaguely breast-shaped light fixtures. He seemed warm and attentive and we began to flirt gently, then more intensely, as the evening went on and he consumed more wine. He moved closer to me on the velvet settee and offered to get us a room at the hotel, and I took him up on it. We made out for a few hours in the stuffy but charming room overlooking the city, and then we left separately.

I continued to see him about once a week after that but only in the evenings and only for a few hours at a time. We enjoyed sex and good conversation, but I was always left wanting more. I was somewhat appeased by our exchange of erotic poetry over the computer. My poems became increasingly emotional while his remained purely sexual, but I didn't want to fully acknowledge this.

One evening Carlton came over with take-out sushi (vegan burdock, hijiki, avocado, and mushroom for me, lots of raw fish for him) from my favorite restaurant, and we sat on my living room floor to eat our picnic. He consumed his tuna roll almost obscenely, and seemed especially skittish, but I ignored this until he said quickly and without punctuation, "Oh by the way did I tell you Kelly is coming to stay with me next week for a month."

I felt a backlog of panic rise up in my body like bile, but I tried to continue on with the conversation we'd been having. However, the upset came out in my tone and soon we were snapping at each other. We had sex anyway and then he left.

A week later I called him and asked if we could talk. I wanted to know why he and Kelly had decided not to divorce, since she lived with her boyfriend and Carlton was in a different country dating other women.

He grew silent on the other end of the phone and when he spoke his voice was perilously tense.

"I don't think it is anyone's business what Kells and I choose to do or choose not to do," he said. "Our relationship isn't something everyone understands but it is what we have. She's my best friend. I'm the only family she has, and she's the only person I really feel comfortable with."

"I don't get it," I said.

"If there was a fire, who would you help first?" he asked, and then went on, before I could begin to answer this strange question: "Your children or your lover? You would choose your children."

I had no idea what he meant. "Okay," I said. "I still don't get it."

"It's none of your business," he replied. "Unless someone is planning to marry me it is none of their business."

I raised my voice when I spoke again. "I think I am at least allowed to ask about this since we're sleeping together."

"You can ask whatever you want but I don't have to answer," he said.

"Why are you being so mean?"

"I don't love you!" he shouted. "Okay? I'm not in love with you."

"Who even says that?" I shouted back. "I didn't ask you if you were in love with me."

We hung up and didn't speak for months. When we finally met again (I know, I know—I was a lonely, bored, over-worked, over-stressed single mom who wanted sex and comfort of some kind) he seemed warm and calm and apologized for his sharp words. We had another lovely evening and ended up in bed.

Just a few weeks later he went to visit Kelly for Christmas in Canada. I contained myself, realizing that this was part of the deal. When he returned he told me they had spent the week in her apartment watching movies, talking, hanging out. He said her boyfriend was upset.

I said, "I can imagine."

His dull and muddied eyes switched on like lights behind his glasses. "Why should he feel upset? I'm the one who should feel upset! She left *me* for *him*!"

For the first time I heard the real passion he still harbored. There was no way to deny it this time. When he told me once again, "I don't love you," slipping and sliding around the floor in his socks, I finally got the message clearly. There was nothing here for me, and we ended it for good.

Why, you may ask, did I spend so much time on this Urban Elf? Someone who would not acknowledge his own shadow, neither in his art nor in his life. Yes, the sex and conversation were enjoyable. Yes, he served as yet another muse, inspiring poetry even after he was gone, but I had lots of other ex-boyfriend muses. I think, in part, my instincts were clouded by more than just the common factors of loneliness and sexual frustration. Just as a shadow would literally obscure my vision a couple of years later, another shadow lived inside of me already.

SUBPLOTS ARE PLOTS, TOO

A subplot, otherwise thought of as a secondary storyline, can provide additional insight into the main character and contribute to furthering the character's arc.

For example, in a book about a drug addict trying to get clean, a subplot might involve a best friend dying of an overdose. This subplot would inform the main character's journey, contributing to the main character's decision to dramatically change.

Subplots don't have to always provide crises; these secondary storylines can also offer moments of reprieve from the tension of the novel. A break from tension offers a kind of suspense in itself: As we are pulled away from the main plot to catch our breath, we may also become breathless again as we wait to see what happens when we return to the main story.

Subplots can be introduced in flashbacks. Flashbacks should escalate the conflict in the same way as all other storylines—they build tension, overtly or subtly, though not always chronologically.

Subplots can also be introduced in exposition, dialogue, stories-within-stories, and lyrical interludes.

I should forget about Internet dating, maybe all dating, I told myself after Carlton, *and just stay home, unplug, and write another book.* Unfortunately, my new project didn't take enough of my energy to keep me from yearning for a relationship, and soon I found myself back online, trying again.

As I dated more frequently, on the nights my children were with their dad, the energy in my home changed, and it seemed the frogs and the fairies had left the garden. The old tree sprouted a lacey white frill of fungus and died, and the flowers withered without its shade.

Life became more complicated a few years later, after my experience with the man who lived in his mother's closet, my vision loss, and my mom's death.

Thank god my children were okay, though the stress of their grandmother's illness and their mom's difficult eye surgery had certainly affected them. (Remember my daughter's elflocks? They symbolized so much of our turmoil.)

Some of my friends, perhaps freaked out by my stroke of bad luck, perhaps by my dating escapades, disappeared from my life. I was having trouble getting writing contracts, and my mortgage rates were astronomical—I'd been (stupidly, on my part) talked into a terrible interest-only loan at the height of the housing crisis and had fallen deeply underwater.

Afraid of losing my home, and my life savings embedded in it, in this flood, I tried to negotiate with the bank, but they "misplaced" my paperwork over and over again, shuffled me around from case manager to case manager, and refused to return my calls, hanging up on me on more than one occasion, in spite of Obama's homeowner protection policies. I stayed up-to-date on my payments, but the situation had become dire.

One of my students started an online petition signed by thousands of my fans (I am ever-grateful) and after a final pleading tweet (take note: banks hate bad press on Twitter), I got a helpful response. The bank eventually modified my loan.

I kept dating after that, but things seemed to grow more ominous. One man I went out with seemed promising at first, if only because he wanted to talk about writing. He recounted a short story he'd written for a class, in which a young boy is graphically mauled and killed by a lawn mower gone awry while his mother obliviously cleans her house.

"The other students told me I couldn't write about that," the man said, stroking his goatee primly. His mouth had a cruel twist I hadn't noticed before. "They insisted I at least have the mother come out and save him."

"You can write anything you want," I told him, but the question was, *why* did he want to? And, more importantly, why was I seeing someone who could talk about a subject like this with such bladelike precision and coldness?

Another man told me the story of how his mother had killed herself and left a note blaming him for her death.

"My sister knew the letter was in the house and let me go there and find it for myself," he told me over dinner at an organic restaurant in Culver City.

This man had a doughy face, a heavy French accent, and, second to the lawn mower man, the coldest eyes I'd ever seen, even in the ambient lighting. Over dinner, the French-man asked me the thirty-six questions that are supposed to make you fall in love with anyone, kissed me in the parking lot with a mouth that tasted of roast beef, told me he wanted to see me again, and then never called me back. I didn't want to see him either but felt disgust with myself for revealing so much to him in those thirty-six questions and then letting him kiss me at all.

Then there was Jupiter. I met him online when he discovered my poetry blog, but he lived across the country and our relationship had always felt purely platonic. He got off the dating site and told me he was seeing someone; we continued to correspond. Eventually, he asked if he could come visit me.

I took a chance and let him, giving him the name of a hotel where he could stay. When he arrived at my door with his pale, bloated face; long, greasy hair; and pinprick eyes, I realized something was very wrong. Instead of making an excuse not to see him, I took him around LA for the next two days, relieved when he finally left. But before he did so, he confided in me that a friend of his had died suddenly, and Jupiter worried he would be blamed. I never inquired further.

Soon after, he sent me a huge sci-fi manuscript he had written out by hand. It was almost illegible and completely incomprehensible. I broke off all contact. A few months later I received a group email announcing his death, with no clear explanation.

Luckily I hadn't been physically harmed by any of these men, but I had certainly managed to put my psyche, at least, in harm's way (though I no longer lived on that street), and my taxonomy of mythic "types" hadn't helped. We were just people after all, not magical creatures. Suffering people. I realized how much I must still have hated myself, on some level, to jeopardize my physical and mental health, for what? For a (slim) chance at romantic love? And after all I'd already gone through?

My masochism had shown up as that ballet master with the cane, hooking my leg; it had shown up as Jaedon, but somehow this new wave of self-harm was different. I was older and more experienced, had been in therapy for years, and ideally should have known better.

A FEW YEARS earlier, I'd attended some Sex Love Addicts Anonymous meetings with my friend Miranda. She'd shown me the SLAA checklist for self-diagnosis and insisted I fit the bill, though I wasn't as sure. But I went with her anyway, to a retreat at a monastery in the hills above Malibu. Maybe I could write about it, I told myself.

Miranda and I shared a room in the mission-style building on the slope above the sea. We went to put our things away, and she pulled off her shirt and bra, revealing her large breasts and smiling at me.

"This is going to be good," she said.

We did yoga and took hikes among wildflowers by day, but I found myself growing uncomfortable at the nightly fireside meetings, talking about sex with strangers, especially the men. Many of these people seemed to come from terribly abusive backgrounds. One unsmiling young woman with an ironic beehive hairdo and horn rim glasses approached me afterward and adopted me as her "sponsee." According to her shares, she'd had a rather horrific experience with sex growing up.

"You have to cut off all contact with all men," she said.

"I don't talk to that many men," I told her. This was before I'd started Internet dating, and I'd already stopped attending the trance dance classes where I'd met Jaedon.

"You can't masturbate any more, at all," my sponsor said.

"That's never interfered with anything," I told her.

"And you have to read these commitments aloud at the next meeting," she said, ignoring me.

"I really don't feel comfortable saying 'masturbate' in front of a room full of sex addict men I don't know," I told her.

"You're unwilling to heal," she insisted.

I decided not to go back to SLAA and to work on my issues with my therapist instead. But the experience made me realize that my tendency toward addictive behavior was deeply rooted.

Yes, this was my shadow. And, I realized, my mother had the same one. She might not have wanted to look at violence on TV, in movies, or in books, she might not have invited people she didn't know to visit her, but she subjected herself to painful relationships with a series of men, so afraid was she of being alone.

And unlike me, my mom hadn't developed the ability to fully transform her experiences into art. After all, she hadn't had a mother-muse like I had. One who wouldn't admit her shadow was much better than none at all.

12 QUESTIONS FOR *THE HOUSE ON MANGO STREET* BY SANDRA CISNEROS

Esperanza, a young Latina growing up in an impoverished Chicago **setting**, **wants** a house.

She **needs** to feel at home wherever she is, and to help others through her ability to tell stories.

Her **gift** is her power of observation.

Her **flaw** is her tendency to look to others to mirror or define her, rather than looking within.

Her **arc** takes her from a child to a young woman, from an observer to a writer with a poetic **style** who will return home to help others.

One of her **antagonists** is Sally, the girl with eyeliner and high heels who entrances Esperanza and then ditches her at a carnival, where a stranger molests her.

This is both the **crisis** and the **climax** of this succinct poem-of-a-story.

Esperanza comes to an internal **resolution** when she dreams of leaving Mango Street, becoming a writer, and eventually returning—as the mysterious "Three Sisters" have instructed—to help "the ones who cannot get out."

The **theme** is alluded to in Esperanza's name: Hope comes through creative expression, and if we find our voice, we will find our true home.

MY SHADOW IS still alive and well. Since My Secret Man had helped me clean the bedroom, a few months after we'd started dating, the room felt different. Two dark wood, marble-topped end tables gone, as well as a few paintings and two dusty dream catchers. The baskets full of receipts, warranties, hair ties, pencils, and extra buttons had been sorted through and discarded. I'd thrown away my mother's old pillows from the bed she died in and replaced them with fresh, down-filled white pillows from Target that My Secret recommended I buy.

One flame flickered safely protected in its glass votive. No more half-burned perfume holiday candles with wicks that flared. No more lopsided, precarious tapers. It felt safer now.

David Bowie sang "Breaking Glass." Every time the song ended (and it's short: only 1:52) My Secret reached for the remote and hit it again.

"Seems to be working," he said with a wry shift of his lips I could just glimpse in the candlelight.

Only later did we realize what the lyrics to that song really are.

It's about disconnection and darkness and pain. Bowie recorded it in Berlin where he was trying to recover from a cocaine addiction that had turned him into a ninety-eight-pound skeleton dabbling in the occult. The singer is breaking glass in his lover's room, like the pale green Bacardi bottle I once shattered in my college boyfriend Thorn's dorm. Bowie's writing an awful something on the carpet. He's telling his lover to both look and not look at the same time. He's not going to touch his lover. His lover has problems. *Who* has problems? the lover might retort.

David Bowie was a wonderful person who, like all of us, had his share of problems. After his death, among all the outpourings of praise, some people called him a pedophile and rapist, though he was never charged with either of these things.

Like many of Bowie's groupies, I went to the Starwood at sixteen, a haze of India Earth bronzer, toxic glitter, and shiny Spandex, to dance to disco in the barny club with the pink neon sign, but my boyfriend Johnny, the guy my parents set me up with, wasn't David Bowie, not even close.

If David Bowie selected me, in my high-waist Chemin de Fer jeans and Bonne Bell lip gloss, out from a gaggle of teen-age groupies; if he took me to the Chateau Marmont or the Beverly Hills Hotel, gave me champagne, changed into a yellow silk kimono covered with red peonies, bent me over, had sex with me, and then slept with me in high-thread-count sheets bleached whiter than his skin, my life would not have been any more traumatic. Or would it? He must have smelled dangerous like cigarettes and as tranquilizing as flowers.

But even though those were different times, and there were plenty of worse traumas for young girls to experience, I certainly wouldn't want my child to have sex with a thirty-year-old rock star, nor, as my agent pointed out when we discussed it, would Bowie have appreciated it if someone that age expressed interest in his teenage daughter.

When I told my therapist, Sofia, about my relationship with Johnny, she mentioned statutory rape and the power dynamic of a man with a car and independence versus a girl who lives at home with her parents, has no sense yet of her identity. A girl who feels unprotected, undervalued, delivered without care into the man's arms.

I know my parents weren't intentionally harming me. AIDS wasn't a factor in those days and the psychological effects of sex between men and underage girls hadn't been explored as thoroughly. My parents truly believed, I think, that what they saw as a "healthy," loving sexual relationship could be beneficial to me in some ways. And things were just different in Los Angeles in the seventies, especially in a bohemian home where a young poet was being groomed, and in the world of rock and roll.

But some damage had clearly been done to my budding self-esteem.

I'M NOT SURE how the fight started. My Secret Man and I had had a good day. We'd visited the genie man in Silver Lake, with more jewelry to sell. We'd had lunch with the money we made. We'd gone home and walked Elphi to a café and talked. My Secret told me he thought he might be able to learn everything there is to know about writing by studying Shakespeare's sonnets the way Katherine Dunn who wrote *Geek Love* studied only grammar books for years and years. He said he was feeling frustrated about his writing, and I listened patiently and tried to encourage him. We came home and he cleaned files from my computer while I made quinoa and brown rice pasta with cashew pesto.

I wanted to go to sleep and he wanted to keep working on the computer. When he finally got under the covers, one of us reached for the other and one of us pulled away.

That's when the demons flooded the room. All the people who hurt us had entered our bed and we screamed back at them.

My Secret got out of bed. "I can't do this," he said. He pulled on his pants. His belt clanked, metal on metal.

> So much of creativity lives in the dark places inside of us. It is our artistic responsibility to mine them for treasure.

I lay there, frozen, like an animal in shock, about to be attacked. My dog pressed his warmth against my leg and I tried to match my breathing to his. In the past I would have just stayed there, paralyzed, my limbs tingling, my organs growing, my whole body expanding, metastasizing, becoming a giantess.

But I wasn't going to do that anymore.

I reached over and turned on the light. I sat up. "We have to stop," I said, keeping my voice modulated so as not to startle any of us further, including the dog. "We're not even talking to each other. We need to look at each other."

Were we enacting some kind of twisted Cupid and Psyche myth? In the actual *marchen*, Venus, the love goddess, envies Psyche and curses her to marry a beast. Instead, Venus's son Cupid rescues her, takes her to his palace of jewels, silver, and citrus wood and makes love to her each night in the darkness.

Her jealous sisters convince her that he is a beast and, doubting her lover, Psyche lights an oil lamp to spy on him, planning to stab the monster with a knife as he sleeps. Startled by his beauty, she spills some wax on his flesh, burning and waking him. He flees. Psyche is cursed to serve Venus with a series of near-impossible tasks until she eventually wins her lover back.

But maybe we'd both become beasts, trapped in our pain.

My Secret slumped down on the bed and blinked at me with bright red eyes, eyes that didn't look like his own, in a swollen face.

Suddenly I felt so tired. It was late and I hadn't been getting enough sleep for weeks. When we couldn't see each other, we stayed up talking on the phone. When we did see each other, I woke up early no matter how late we turned off the light. I wanted to fall into the mattress, fall through to another world, never come back.

In the morning I woke raw, flayed. Up too early again. I got out of bed as quietly as I could so as not to wake him. I took a bath, shaved my legs, walked the dog, forced down a smoothie, did some writing. Then I wrote an apologetic letter.

When he got up we hugged tentatively and I resisted the urge to disaffectedly (vindictively?) pat his shoulders instead of squeezing them. I asked him what he wanted to do. Suggested he take a shower, get something to eat and drink before we talked. He didn't have clean clothes with him so he said maybe we could go to Target, he could buy T-shirts and underwear and take a shower and then go to our café.

We did this. A good plan. First things first. Hot water, clean clothes; then coffee, bread.

On the way to coffee, he read the email and said, "Thank you for writing this."

"I wanted to try and make it better," I said.

And then, somehow, we were fighting again. All the emotion from the night before came back like a pump of adrenaline in my veins.

We parked near our café by the house with the giant pelican statue in front. Its huge gullet disturbed me. I don't remember what was said except that by the end I was hitting the steering wheel and he was getting out of the car, slamming the door on the metal seatbelt buckle, and walking away.

I drove past the D*Face mural of the motorcycle with the green Frankenstein monster and hot, crying blond, tiny horns made of clouds peeking out of her hair. I forced myself to go to the gym, and then I called My Secret and asked him if he wanted to see my therapist Sofia with me.

"I can't," he said.

I drove to Sofia, over the freeways to her office in a shady bungalow in Pasadena. The light has a greenish tinge from all the trees.

After one breakup with a man I'd been dating, I'd called Sofia, sobbing. I was walking around the little park by my house, a rectangle of grass lined by jacaranda and eucalyptus trees with a playground, tennis courts, basketball court, and stone house where my children went to preschool.

She'd said, "You sound like you're dying." It felt that way. She'd asked, "Is it like when you were a baby, with the meningitis?"

I'd had a fever that led to a seizure and my mom rushed me to the hospital, leaving the front door open, terrifying my eight-year-old brother Zack, who came home to an abandoned house.

The veins in my arms were too small for the needle, so the doctor used my ankles. I have tiny seams there, still (though fading among the marks of age), neatly sewn. (I used to pretend they were the scars left from amputated wings.) My mom couldn't stay; I was left in the dark alone, waiting to be sucked back into the vortex I had so recently emerged from.

When I wasn't taken away, I think I began to wonder if I deserved life. How could I pay back this debt? *Write, write, write a hundred books. And find someone to love you, someone to reassure you you are not alone, you are wanted, you are here.*

Because Sofia caught me in that moment of terror, because she remained steady as I relived the loss, because of the years of her always being present and so profoundly kind, something shifted. I have never since felt that same sensation of dying after a breakup—the pure abandonment of self.

"Remember, misattunements happen all the time. It's how we repair them," she said when I left her office.

THE NEXT TIME I saw My Secret Man we went to our vegan Thai place. Once, I admired the waitress, Summer's pale pink lip gloss and she gave me the empty box to try to find the right shade. That night she had on orange eye shadow like an LA summer sunset. She brought us our usual curries and my Gingeraid kombucha.

My Secret and I surveyed each other across the table. The large yellow gerbera daisy in the vase covered one of his eyes.

"I'm sorry," I said. My throat had a little heart, the size of a lamprocapnos flower, throbbing inside of it.

"I'm sorry too," he said, leaning forward so I could see both eyes bleuried with emotion. "I think we're both just afraid. We both wanted this kind of intimacy so much. We were scared, too. I think that's why all that happened."

Did I fear intimacy? I always said how much I wanted it. But with my own self-doubts, with the awful, unseen words of self-hate scrawled upon the floor, with my broken shards of glass, I was pushing him away as I'd done with others so many times before.

I'm not doing this anymore, I told myself.

I'm not breaking glass with this man.

He'd cleaned the pain and clutter from my house. Listened to my tales of trauma and offered comfort. Read my tales of trauma and offered advice. Played Bowie when the silence in the room turned cold. Held me in his arms.

Like David Bowie says, we have our problems, our shadows, certainly. But we're wonderful people, too.

SINCE THAT TIME I've continued to work hard in therapy, in yoga classes and my acupuncturist's office, and at my computer, trying to acknowledge, accept, and understand my shadow. Even if some of my stories might have scared my mother, I know she would, ultimately, be proud of me for facing the dark truth of my psyche.

I've also planted a jacaranda tree in my garden, in her honor, where the old shade tree used to stand. The jacaranda provides almost the same shelter and purple flowers burst from castanet-shaped pods in the spring. My son Sam and I try to sneak up on the frogs that croak by the pond, but we can never catch a glimpse; still we know they're back, for a few months every year, chirruping like gruff angels.

And the fairies have returned as well. My friend's sylph-like daughter with her tilted mirror-blue eyes and Rapunzel hair came over "to see Queen Mab," and we left the little people berries in doll-sized tea cups, a bathtub abalone bowl, and a conch shell to sleep in. By morning the berries were gone and a few rose petals strewn about, though none grow that near. Maybe there are magical creatures after all, just not trolling the Internet.

> Like David Bowie says, we have our problems, our shadows. But we're wonderful people, too.

Perhaps they're waiting to have their stories told.

If I look into the pond, among the purple water lilies, I can see my face reflected amid the leaf-shaped shadows of their eyes.

SO MUCH OF creativity lives in the dark places inside of us. I feel it is almost our artistic responsibility to mine them for treasure. In doing so, we will often find great personal catharsis, and the opportunity to help others face the darkness where creation lives.

THE 12 QUESTIONS: CRISIS
Question #10: What is the crisis of your book?

DURING A STORY'S **crisis**, also known as a character's "dark night of the soul," the character is tested in the most extreme way and may feel ready to surrender. Then the character will summon some courage, make a decision, take action, and push past the threatening obstacle to reach the climax.

It can be easy to confuse the crisis of the book with the climax. The climax occurs as a single moment and scene; the crisis can unfold over a period of escalating tension. For more about climax, turn to page 249.

Here are some examples of **crisis** from our classic books:

In *To Kill a Mockingbird*, the shooting of Tom Robinson serves as a crisis as it exposes Scout to the corruption of the world.

The crisis sequence in *The Great Gatsby* begins with the luncheon in which Tom realizes that Daisy is still in love with Gatsby, and it ends with Daisy killing Myrtle.

In *Jane Eyre*, a crisis begins when Jane is about to marry Rochester but discovers he is already betrothed to Bertha. This is followed by a literal "dark night of the soul" as she wanders the moors, battered by rain and wind.

In *Wuthering Heights*, Catherine's death marks the beginning of a crisis for Heathcliff. His subsequent cruelty toward the other characters reflects his interior dark night.

In *Lolita*, Lolita's illness and subsequent abduction send Humbert into his crisis.

The abortion in *Play It As It Lays* is the inciting incident for Maria's crisis, one that escalates when she realizes that nine months have passed since the aborted baby's conception.

The biggest crisis of a book almost always comes in the later part of the story, after there has been sufficient time for tension to build to a heightened pitch. An extensive, developed crisis helps writers avoid what best-selling author Jim Butcher calls "the great swampy middle." To avoid that daunting bog, make an effort to continually escalate the conflict: Have things get worse, and then worse again, for your character. Allow for some moments of reprieve, but always return the character to another challenge or obstacle, until the moment of climax sets the character up for the ultimate test of his resiliency.

OUR CHARACTERS GROW most through conflict, and by writing about their conflicts, we grow as writers. And as humans.

9

ROUGH MAGICK
—— Love

I N *BIRD BY BIRD*, ANNE LAMOTT SUGGESTS WRITING your books for someone you love instead of for an unknown, and potentially judgmental, audience. The emphasis then falls on emotion and expression rather than on commoditization. Each book can be seen, simply, as a gift.

For me, love and writing have always been one and the same. They both originate within. They are often birthed out of pain, or some kind of sacrifice. They have the potential to create something out of nothing, or transform something, or someone, into something, or someone, else. They don't come easy.

"MOM, DAVID BOWIE died," my daughter Jasmine said. Seven in the morning on January 11, 2016, and she was supposed to be getting ready for school, not on her phone reading about pop culture news, but I was too tired to argue with her. I'd been up since six staring at the computer screen, trying to write bad erotic romance ebooks to pay the bills until I could shake myself out of a year-long creative slump.

The wing of black liner that she had swept expertly above the deep-set blue of her eyes made her appear older than her fifteen years, as she looked up at me briefly from the secret world of her phone. With so many screens around, we almost never really look into each other's eyes anymore.   I admired her high forehead and heart-shaped face, framed by Botticelli Venus hair. She so resembles my mother, who'd died five years before.

"No, it was just his birthday," I said, thinking Jasmine had misread something. I'd been putting up the Helen Green GIF of Bowie on my social media in celebration of his sixty-ninth year: Davy, Ziggy, Thin White Duke, Halloween Jack, Aladdin Sane, Button Eyes, The Preacher, Dark Star. He'd just released a new album. *Black Star.* I'd heard a cut on KCRW. So good.

But Jasmine was insistent.

I Googled his name. His son with Angie, Duncan, had confirmed Bowie's death. Bowie had died of cancer in his home the day before.

Mother fucking cancer. You motherfucker.

"I'm sorry, Mommy," my daughter said. She didn't even glance at her phone. She was looking right at me.

LATER THAT EVENING, my son Sam posed in tribute to Bowie, one hand at his heart, one hand pointed skyward, embodying Bowie on the cover of *Heroes*. They both have high cheekbones, angular jaws, but my son's skin is tan from the California sun, and Bowie pale against the shadowy background.

"Can we watch the video?" Sam asked.

David Bowie is so young and glamorous, standing there in a beam of light. He's both romance and apocalypse, singing my favorite song of all time, the one I always put on every top ten list and make out mix.

Sam and I did sit-ups on the floor while Elphi tried to lick our cheeks, and Bowie sang.

When the song ended, Sam looked at me with those green eyes shining feelings under thickly feathered black eyebrows.

"Would you please put on 'Starman' now, Mom?"

While it played, I heard David Bowie's otherworldly voice in my head, sending me a message.

Text him. That man you met last year.

So I did.

> Love and writing have always been one and the same. They originate within. They have the potential to create something out of nothing. They don't come easy.

I'M GOING TO tell you how I first met My Secret Man, and found him again after Bowie died. But first I want to share a short story I wrote before that. It should give you a little insight into why I ran from love's rough magick the first time around.

The story is written in three different points of view—first, second, and third. Each POV uniquely expresses the protagonist's increasing loss of self as she faces the pain of unrequited love. These variations in perspective are intended to disorient the reader and help her to glean the protagonist's sense of disassociation by observing it from different angles.

THE SPELL
First Person

I know I have to let X go. He's married and has three children. He says he will never be able to leave.

I met him in a novel-writing class I was teaching. When he came up to introduce himself and tell me that he was a fan of my work, I felt the air electrify. I can never remember experiencing anything this strong with a man in the first moment. After my divorce, when I briefly attended Love Addicts Anonymous meetings, I was warned about this. The Book said to turn the other way when you feel that shock with someone. I didn't understand. It was what I'd always been looking for. It's what I thought love was supposed to feel like.

X isn't much taller than I am. Broad shoulders tug the fabric of his shirt. Behind his glasses his eyes are blue. When he laughs, his teeth show—crooked, wild. He wears a golden wedding band.

But X's story for my class was about a man in an unhappy marriage, who feels he can't leave because he has to protect his children. X was an actor and when he read his story out loud I had to hide my tears.

There was a mirthless young woman in the class who really seemed to hate me. She would always challenge everything I said. On the last day, she got really angry because I told another student it was okay to write from more than one point of view in the same piece.

"I thought you said you wanted us to stay close to the character's thoughts and feelings." She was actually fuming.

"Well, it depends on the effect you're going for," I said. "Sometimes it's okay to switch or to create distance. There aren't strict rules. Usually there should be a metaphorical reason behind your choices, but you might not be aware of what it is at first. Your subconscious is dictating the choice and it may be the right one, so go with it at first at least."

"But I have to know the rules before I can break them," she said.

X met her fearsome gaze. "I think that the lessons so far are the best way of showing the 'rules,'" he said. "But it's not a science."

She got up and left the room, dragging my reputation and evaluation points with her like a clattering string of tin cans.

"Well then," X said. Everyone laughed and everything was okay again.

He smiled at me, and so much blood pumped through my body that I was afraid he could hear the rush of it under my skin, even from a few feet away where he sat. I realized how desperate I'd been, after my divorce and the death of my parents, for someone to come to my rescue, though I liked to pretend it wasn't true.

After class X asked if I wanted to go for tea. I experienced a pulse of sensation I didn't recognize at first, until I realized it was joy. As we sat across from each other in the little bougainvillea-walled courtyard café, he told me that he and his wife fought all the time but he couldn't leave. Like the man in his story he didn't want to be away from his kids.

I said I understood. I'd had to go on antidepressants to leave my ex-husband. The thought of even one night away from my children made me literally feel like I was dying. But it had turned out okay. My kids were now away at college and doing well. My ex and I were friendly. I was off the antidepressants.

X nodded but didn't say anything; I could tell this hadn't reassured him.

Water splashed in a cracked stone fountain. My joy had turned to melancholy. But when we said goodbye he hugged me, and I forgot everything but the feel of his shoulders.

X and I saw each other for lunch at the same café a few times a month after the class ended. Once, I said, "Is it just me, or is there something between us here?"

He looked into my eyes, blushed, and nodded.

I said, "Glad we got that cleared up," and we laughed. We didn't talk about it again, though we exchanged emails and still met for lunch sometimes.

He was also the first person I called when I had to go for a follow-up mammogram because the doctor had some questions about the first one.

"My mom died of breast cancer," I told X.

"I'll go with you," he said. And then, with complete conviction: "It'll be okay."

AFTER THE MAMMOGRAM I went out into the waiting room. X looked at me when I walked toward him. He lifted his chin and squinted at me, as if to ask a question. I gave him a thumbs up. He smiled, showing his rowdy teeth, and hugged me.

"Thank you for coming," I said as we walked to the car.

"I understand." X then told me that his father had died of skin cancer. He said it matter-of-factly, as if trying not to draw too much attention.

My short-lived relief changed back to fear. I reached to touch X's shoulder, probably more to reassure myself

than him, but drew my hand away before I'd made contact. Longing shot up my arm like nerve pain. "When's
the last time you went for a check?" I asked.

He cleared his throat and looked away at some pigeons
pecking trash on the sidewalk. "I'm overdue."

I tried to imagine not having X in my life. He had
already become the person I called to go with me to my
mammogram appointment, the person I'd thought of
to help steady me as the cold metal plate had flattened
my breast.

That was when I knew how much I needed him, how
devastated I'd be without him.

I reached for the cell phone in his pocket, this time not
bothering to avoid the electric jolt of touch, and put the
phone in his hand. "I want you to make an appointment
right now," I said. What I was really saying was, "I love you."

NOTHING CHANGED BETWEEN US, though I kept hoping
it would. We never talked about our feelings for each
other. When we went for lunch, he always wore the gold
wedding band. Part of me was hoping he'd remove it, just
for an hour, and then I felt guilty for wanting this.

One time I emailed him and said, "I'm thinking of trying online dating."

"Good idea," he emailed back. "I think you need to
find someone available who can really be there for you
and give you all you deserve."

I had my answer, in writing. It didn't matter that I loved him, or even how much. I had to let him go.

I go to see my friend the Oracle. She lives with her husband in a Craftsman house in East LA. It's the night before my birthday. I've brought some items with me, according to her general instructions calling for "stones, flowers, symbols of meaning." In my case: a piece of rose quartz, a pink rose, a crystal phallus, a tiny sculpture of a goddess that my father, the artist, made many years ago before he got too sick to work.

I get lost in the rain on the way to the Oracle. My Waze app keeps taking me to the same house over and over again, but it's not hers. The address isn't even close. I call the Oracle and she gives me directions, but I get lost three more times before I find her. When I finally arrive it's raining harder and I'm crying. I've just heard a story on the radio about a college student who wandered onto a freeway, drunk and disoriented, and was hit by a car. His body was destroyed beyond recognition.

I take off my rain-soaked jacket and the Oracle hugs me. Her arms are strong and warm.

{ I always get lost in the rain on the way to the Oracle. My Waze app keeps taking me to the wrong address. }

I follow the feline sway of her hips upstairs to an attic room that smells of herbs and beeswax. Candles burn on a low table.

I tell the Oracle about X, secretly hoping she will suggest some magic to make him leave his wife.

"That's black magic. I can't do that."

"Oh," I say. "I'm sorry!"

"But we could do a cord-cutting ceremony to let him go."

For some reason I think of Joni Mitchell, who is in a coma in a hospital. Joni has this disease called Morgellons, in which fibers appear under the surface of the skin, making it itch and crawl. No one knows what the fibers are or what causes them to be there. Many doctors don't believe the disease is real. It strikes me as particularly horrible that Joni Mitchell has to suffer with this. She had polio as a child. That's how she wrote that song about wishing for a river to skate away on. Some people can transform shit into beauty.

The Oracle's voice is deep and mellifluous as she beats a drum and calls on the spirits to come and bless us. Her hand is so large it completely covers the skin head of the drum. In the candlelight she looks like a tall French actress, with her effortlessly tousled bob, the gap between her teeth, her lambent eyes. She opens the window and little gusts of wind scatter shards of rain into the room. The wind becomes my dead mother's spirit caressing my face. Longing beats me like a hand drum. Tears trickle onto my rain-flecked cheeks.

To do the cord cutting I have to write a goodbye note to X, releasing him from any romantic entanglements with me. I tell the Oracle I don't want to release all entanglements because X and I are good friends, and "I don't want to completely lose him." She doesn't love this but I remind her that X and I have never slept together or even kissed. Once the back of his hand accidentally brushed against my breast when we were fighting over the check at lunch and my previously hibernating nipple came to life, but I don't tell her that.

Dear X,
Thank you for being my friend, for always answering
my emails, for taking me to lunch, for defending me
in class, for going with me to get the mammogram, for
your hugs. I want to keep our friendship strong, but I
need to give up the hope of it becoming more. I release
you from any romantic ties to me. I wish you every
blessing and all love.

After the cord cutting I can't stop crying. The Oracle suggests she throw in a love spell to help bring true love into my life or at least cheer me up. So I agree, thanking her, and she has me write a love note to my beloved, listing all his traits. Trying not to think of X, I write, "You are kind, wise, compassionate, loving, sexy, stable, strong, creative, a liberal, and a feminist. You share my interests. We have a powerful sexual attraction and spiritual connection." Thinking clearly of X, I add, "You are not romantically tied to anyone else." The Oracle folds up the note and draws some runes on it. We put it in a little gauze pouch along with the pink rose petals, the rose quartz, the goddess, and the crystal fascinum. I tie the bag three times and we say an incantation.

We go downstairs to the kitchen. The Oracle's husband is making a Thai stir fry. Like the Oracle, he is tall and catlike, but while she has the eyes of a mystic, his gaze is very much in the present, reflecting his wife and her friend, the Thai food, the rain that strikes the shingles.

The Oracle summoned her husband to her with a spell. The same spell she and I performed tonight.

He kisses her, his hands on her hips, and their love is as tangible as the smell of ginger, garlic, and lemongrass. The Oracle and her husband ask if I would like to stay for dinner. I thank them, but I'm eager to be alone with the aftereffects of my spell.

The Oracle and I go into the backyard. It's overgrown and the rain has soaked the unmowed lawn, but the showers have stopped. We light a candle and I burn the goodbye letter to X. The flames leap toward me as if they don't want to let me go. As if they want to consume me.

I take the ashes with me, "To release at a crossroads," the Oracle instructs.

On the way home I stop at an intersection where the streetlights have gone out. I guess the storm downed a power line somewhere.

Never step in water near a downed line.

The intersection is dark and deserted. Dangerous in more ways than one. I get out carefully and scatter the ashes from a glass jar into the wet night. They cling to my hands and brush against my lips. I taste like fire but no one will know except me.

I get back in the car, drive home, put the charm under my pillow, and sleep.

The next day, my birthday, my three best girlfriends, who all happen to be poets, former ballerinas, and Pisces, the wisest sign, take me out for brunch at our favorite restaurant. We eat waffles with strawberries and whipped cream and drink green tea bobas. I tell them about the love spell and the cord cutting, and they all think it's good I'm letting go of X but that I should be careful not to get carried away with the love spell part.

When I arrive home I see that a man from FU Cupid has contacted me. An architect, a surfer, divorced, and has a kid in college. Lives nearby. We speak on the phone and his voice is deep and warm. It turns out we even went to the same university, and at the same time. We share the same favorite book that we both read in our freshman year. *One Hundred Years of Solitude*. It changed my life because of the magic and his because of the realism. I email the Oracle and say, "I think the charm is working."

"That's great!" she says. "But wait and see."

Second Person

You go to coffee with the architect, Z. He's as good looking in person as in his pictures. There are more lines visible on his forehead, but they make him even more attractive; they show he is a worrier like you. You're both parents, after all. Worry is a prerequisite.

Z and you talk about your children, your work, the school you both went to. You're both liberal, spiritual but not religious, obsessed with music. When you're about to leave, he hugs you and says, "I really want to see you again."

"I'd love to," you say. Your heart is that pink rose you brought to the Oracle's house. The love charm is working. So is the cord cutting. You're not even thinking about X anymore. He's just your friend, that's all.

Z takes you out for dinner at your favorite restaurant. He orders some wine and looks into your eyes across the candle flames. You don't once think of the fire that burned your letter to X.

Z says, "I want my next relationship to last the rest of my life," and your heart leaps toward him like the flames that burned the letter.

After dinner Z walks you to your car that you've parked on the roof in case there's chemistry between you. You can see the twinkling lights of your little downtown; palm trees and jacaranda trees; the angular brick hotel where the Munchkins stayed when they were shooting *The Wizard of Oz*.

Z kisses you goodnight. It's a little awkward but you think that's pretty typical. You get in your car and drive down to the bottom of the parking lot. You see him running over to your car. You roll down the window, and he leans in and kisses you again. It's better this time, melty and sweet like the vanilla ice cream on the Apple Betty you shared for dessert because he said it was his favorite. You grab his chin, which feels a little scratchy and rough, and he puts his hand in your hair. You're wet and excited and you go home and touch yourself and think about him. You don't think about X even once.

You have another date with Z very much like the first one except this time you make out in his Mini Cooper for a while before you go inside. It's hard to really do much because his car is small and his legs are long but you rub his surf-sculpted chest through his light blue cotton shirt and he holds your neck and touches your thighs and you are both smiling even as you kiss and kiss.

The third date you do something you really shouldn't do so soon: You invite Z to your house for dinner. He comes over wearing a white dress shirt and carrying a bouquet of pink lilies and a bottle of rosé wine that Brad Pitt and Angelina Jolie make at their French chateau. He kisses you at the door, just brushing his lips against yours, tantalizing you, and you tug on the sleeve of his shirt a little when he hugs you, to release some of the excitement in your body.

Z and you listen to Arcade Fire, The Black Keys, and the Silversun Pickups ("Test: Do you know why they're

{ If writing is love, does that make writer's block the opposite? }

called that?" he asks, and you say, "That's a crossroads in Silver Lake," and he says, "Yes! You passed the test!") while you set the table with the botanical floral wedding china you got to keep after the divorce and your mother's gold-rimmed wine glasses and serve the dinner you've made. Baked salmon with a honey mustard and lemon sauce, a green salad with pumpkin seeds and cranberries, and butternut squash soup. He says it's delicious, staring into your eyes like he's talking about something else, and you take a sip of the pale pink wine and your whole body thrums with the liquid and the words. For dessert you've made Apple Betty from an old handwritten cookbook of your mom's. It's not as good as the one from the restaurant—the oats and brown sugar are a little dry—but the apples are still warm and moist and the vanilla ice cream reminds you of the first time Z kissed you.

After dinner you sit on the couch and talk. He shows you a picture of a home he built for his parents—a three-story building made mostly of glass and some redwood with a cylindrical glass tower overlooking the sea. When you were a little girl you used to draw pictures of cylindrical glass houses all the time but you don't tell Z this. He is talking anyway, telling you he's very close to his mother and father. He says, "This might be too much information, but the next relationship I'm in, I want it to be with someone who can help me through the death of my parents."

You think, *This is something I can do. This is something I've been through. My loss has prepared me.*

He tells you that the reason he broke up with his last girlfriend was because she didn't want to take it further, that they had fun together but that he's looking for something serious and long lasting.

Then he kisses you, and it's not awkward at all. He tastes like sunshine and the sea. He looks deep into your eyes and says, "You're so beautiful. I love your smile." He gently slips the straps of your pink silk camisole off your shoulders and stares at your breasts and says, "You have such a beautiful body." He kisses your breasts and then unbuttons your jeans and slides them off. He strokes your lips, parts them, puts his finger inside you and says, "Can you come this way?" You shake your head, no, though it feels like you almost could this time. He says, "I want to lick you," and you're nervous because you haven't had a bikini wax for over a month; you didn't expect to get undressed with him yet, even though you did invite him over for dinner on the third date. But you let him lick you. It feels good but you're still too nervous to come. You put your fingers between your legs and touch yourself while you lie in his arms and he kisses you, taking away your inhibitions with a mouth that still tastes of you. When you finally come you both sigh. You ask what you can do for him. He says, "You just did." But then he's sitting on top of you and you're unzipping him and taking his penis out.

You do not once think of X.

The spell is working.

The next night you get an email saying that Z has spent the day reading one of your novels and that your mind is as beautiful as your smile. You make plans for the following weekend, which happens to be Valentine's Day. Like a teenager, you plan your outfit and make a music playlist for Z and listen to it over and over. *The magic is working.*

A few days later you get another email from Z. You only really notice one word at first. The word is *regret*. Your heart drops to your stomach like a bag of stones. You read the email. It says that he ran into an ex-girlfriend at a party the night after you were together. They'd gone out a few years ago but she'd been in the middle of a divorce so the timing wasn't right. At the party she was flirting with him. He told her that he'd met someone and she interrupted him and asked him to get back together with her. He says he had to think about it because of how much he likes you. But "those months with her were among the best of my life." So he decided to try things with her again. (The girlfriend who didn't want to take things further?) He says, "I felt it wouldn't be fair to you, me, or her if I didn't try."

You get in bed and try to read *The Shadow of the Wind*, a mystery about the wonder of books, but you were going to recommend it to Z so you can't concentrate. Your stomach churns with a gelatinous liquid. You keep thinking about his fingers inside of you. Was he testing you out? You remember how he asked if you could come that way—meaning vaginally. Was that part of his decision to go with the ex-girlfriend instead of you? What else did he find wanting? Was there even an ex-girlfriend at all? Or maybe there was a girlfriend and she cast a spell. *Witch*, you call her, and then remember that you cast one, too. She was just better at it.

You try to sleep. The love charm under your pillow just feels like a pouch of sharp rocks. You take it out and look. Through the sheer gauze you see that the tiny goddess is broken clean in half.

In a month you will learn that the Oracle has left her husband.

Third Person

In the morning the woman calls her three Pisces girlfriends and they comfort her and plan a Valentine's dinner together. They go for sushi and then to a sex store to buy vibrators. She goes home, but she can't sleep. She wants to leave her body. She uses her new vibrator while listening to the sex soundtrack she made for Z, but it reminds her of him too much, and she can't come even though the new vibrator is top notch because her girlfriends are always right.

She texts X.

They go out for lunch at their favorite cafe. X hugs her and she feels the strong, comforting muscles of his back. The way their bodies would fit together—hollow to swell, swell to hollow—if they were lying down. The warmth of his skin. She loves his skin—she has comforted herself with the thought of it, lusted after it, worried about it—though she hasn't seen or felt much of it.

She and X sit under a shade umbrella by a fountain. The waiter brings their salads. Pink bougainvillea blossoms drop onto the table and scatter like crumpled bits of tissue paper.

X says, "You look sad. Or something?"

She tells X about what happened with Z.

X frowns. "He obviously doesn't deserve you," he says, which is what all her girlfriends said, too. They also said that about X. Then he tells her that he's been fighting with his wife nonstop. He says, "I stayed for my kids. But now I think it was a mistake. I don't think it's good for them."

She starts to cry; she can't help it. "I'm sorry," she says, turning away. "I tried to forget about you. But it didn't work." He is everything she wished for, except available. He is the essence of rose petals and rose quartz; he is the crystal phallus and the goddess muse. But she is broken.

His eyes fill with tears, too. "I'm sorry," he says.

When he walks her to her car she looks into his eyes and it's as if the sky is shining directly through them, the exact same shade of lit blue coming through. He reaches for her and hugs her close.

There is no severing between them.

She no longer believes in magic.

Can you identify the 12 Questions in this story?

What is this character's **gift**? That she believes in magic? What is her **flaw**? That she deludes herself? What is her **want**?

Love? What is her **need**? To face reality? Who are her (external) **antagonists**? X and Z. What is her **arc**?

In a short story, as opposed to a novel, the writer doesn't have time to take a character along the full trajectory of her arc. But the writer can show the character at a point where she is about to change. In *Writing in General and the Short Story in Particular*, Rust Hills, former *Esquire* editor and husband of the author Joy Williams, talks about ending a short story at a **crisis** or **crossroads**. While a novel slowly builds to the **crisis** of the book and takes the character through it to the **climax** and **resolution**, a short story often depicts only a small part of the crisis and leaves us wondering how it will be resolved.

What is the **theme** of my short story? That we will suffer if we live in delusion and look to things outside of us for help, rather than relying on ourselves?

As mentioned, the jarring **stylistic** shift from first person, to second, to third, shows the character becoming less and less in touch with herself. The use of the letters X and Z for the men is also meant to reflect disconnect.

A couple of final questions to ask about this character:

First: What the fuck is wrong with her?

And: Did she ever learn to believe in magic again? The real kind, the kind that comes from hard work, patience, and self-awareness?

To find out, let's look at what happened after the events loosely described in this story occurred:

A man found me on FU Cupid. When I told him I'd written a punk rock Los Angeles fairy tale, he guessed who I was before he'd learned my name.

He stood in the parking lot in front of the vegan restaurant, leaning on the tractor (that's supposed to make customers think of farms but just made him laugh), arms folded over broad chest, long legs crossed. We'd already had a silly conversation about personal style, how, according to some women's magazine he'd read in a doctor's office, it can possibly determine the potential of relationships. He wore a black T-shirt, denim jacket and jeans, and black Converse; I wore white skinny jeans, a black tank top, a denim jacket and black ankle boots. We sat under the full moon, the same color as his hair. The sky turned shades of blue jean dark, making the moon glow brighter, and we shared a kale salad and a pizza and talked about writing.

> He really, really wanted to write, maybe more than anyone I'd ever met—I could feel it like a third presence at our table.

I told him that although I rarely suffered from writer's block ("and with a last name like mine, I never use the term"), lately I'd been stuck, that I was struggling to get a book contract, to reinvent myself, to figure out what I wanted to write. Meanwhile, I told him, I'd been churning out romances under a pen name to pay the bills.

"Why don't you write a memoir?" he suggested. "I bet your fans would love to hear about your life growing up in Los Angeles."

Two other smart friends of mine had recently said the same thing. "You're pretty good at coming up with ideas," I said to the man across the table from me.

"For other people," he said. "And even for myself I guess. I just can't write them down. And if I do, I give up on them."

He really, really wanted to write, maybe more than anyone I'd ever met—I could feel it like a third presence at our table. I wanted to help him but I wasn't sure how.

"Another weird thing," he said, changing the subject. "I read about your eye surgery online. I had something similar."

When he was nine, a kid threw a spoon down from a tree and it hit my date in the eye and tore his retina. He had to stay in a hospital with both eyes bandaged and his mother only came to visit once. A cataract had formed, making him nearly blind in that eye.

I told him more about my vitrectomy.

We went on to talk about souls.

"When my children were born I felt as if I'd been searching for them my whole life," I said.

"You just really wanted kids?"

"No. I was searching for their particular souls. I know it sounds crazy." I didn't say that there was only one soul still missing from my life.

He walked me to my car, standing to my left so we could see each other better.

"Good eye, good eye," he said.

"Are you Australian?" I asked. I thought this was very funny.

I held onto his arm for support. I was about to go in for foot surgery in a few days. The operation was called a cheilectomy. The doctor would make a zig-zagged incision and shave down the arthritic spur on my big toe so bone would no longer grind relentlessly against bone.

The man texted me when I got home. *I liked talking to you about writing and eyes and souls. I liked when you took my arm in the parking lot. I still smell your perfume on me.*

My fragrance, from my friend Denise Hamilton the mystery writer and perfume guru, tells the story of a woman and her Spanish lover during the Holy Week in Spain—orange blossoms and lavender and frankincense and myrrh.

This man sent me his short stories. They were brief and lyrical with a strangeness that I admired. A man dates a woman who keeps a parrot on her headboard while she has sex. A stripper spends all of her boyfriend's money. A woman has sex with an ex-boyfriend and then stands basking naked in the light from her refrigerator. After her mother's funeral, a young woman encounters a man without an eye. A man is swindled out of his inheritance and invents a soft drink. Most of the stories were about the difficulty of relationships. When I read the descriptions of the women, I was sad that none of them seemed to resemble me in any way. Even though none of the relationships worked out, I wanted to resemble the women, at least one of them. I wanted to be the women the writer imagined in his head before he met me.

Whether he'd imagined me or not, he wanted to see me again.

And though I thought he might be that missing soul I'd been searching for my whole life, I said no.

He wondered if it was because I thought he was only interested in me as a writer. "I'm sorry I talked so much about writing," he emailed. "I just get very excited about it because it's all so new to me and I admire that you've done it for so long. I want you to know that I like you because I'm interested in you as a woman. There was something magical about that night with the moon."

He was right about the magic. But the talk about writing wasn't the reason I didn't go out with him again. My foot would be sawed open in a few days. Years before, I'd let a man I didn't really know help me through the vitrectomy and it had literally led to madness. I still hadn't recovered from the failed spell. Apparently, there were quite a few things I needed to figure out.

> This man sent me his short stories. They were brief and lyrical with a strangeness that I admired.

THE 12 QUESTIONS FOR DAVID BOWIE

Let's imagine we are writing a book about David Bowie. How would a narrative story about Bowie answer the 12 Questions?

> Bowie, the main **character**, is a shape-shifter whose **gift** allows him to enchant and creatively seduce the people he meets. They fall helplessly under his spell—his glamour in the archaic sense, as well as his very real glamour. This mutability sometimes harms his close relationships and ultimately leads to his **flaw**: an urge toward self-destruction.

Bowie might **want** to change as a way to connect to as many people as possible, and to achieve astronomical fame. But how can he really connect with others if he is always shifting shape?

Bowie **needs** the deep connection to himself, his art, and his family. Perhaps this is the result of a **childhood wound** of being born into a family that didn't understand him, and where schizophrenia was rampant, leading to the death of his older half-brother.

Bowie's **arc** could follow his own evolution, from extreme shape-shifter art alien to skeletal, occult-obsessed drug addict, to connected human husband and father, and perhaps an even more realized artist.

An **antagonist** might be a Mephistophelean record label executive, an evil drug dealer, an exploitative talk show host, or rabid fans—anyone who wanted to use, abuse, and ultimately destroy Bowie. An internal antagonist would be his feeling of isolation, leading to addiction.

The **setting** could be expansive—from Brixton, England, to Manhattan, New York, with his beloved wife and daughter, with scenes in Canada, Japan, China, Australia, Europe, the Netherlands, Eastern Europe, the Bahamas. Or, the setting could be condensed to Hollywood, New York, and Berlin, where Bowie and his friend and collaborator Iggy Pop went to get clean.

The **style** and **imagery** might be as varied as the man himself. The **voice** could also change as each of Bowie's personas evolves, and just as his music did on his different albums.

There are many opportunities to introduce **crisis** into Bowie's story: an appearance on TV, when he is clearly high on cocaine; the death of a close friend from drugs; an encounter with a rival who wants to undermine Bowie's success; a disagreement with a music executive who controls Bowie's creative fate.

The **theme** could be that if one learns to connect with oneself and a beloved few, then the sense of isolation will dissipate and the connection to the broader world will strengthen.

The **resolution** would reunite Bowie with his true love, ready to start a family. ══════════════

MAYBE NOW, NINE months later, the day after Bowie's death, it was too late.

The man's phone number was still in my cell; I must have known I'd call him eventually, though I had no idea if he'd answer.

I tentatively asked if he wanted to come to my reading in a few weeks.

Sure, he texted.

Then I asked him if he'd like to have coffee Friday night.

I can't that night, he answered.

My heart weighed as much as my head. Maybe he was dating someone.

How about tonight? I asked anyway.

Yes.

We met for coffee at the café of a restaurant in downtown Culver City across from the hotel where the Munchkins stayed. It's rumored that they got drunk and swung from the fire escapes.

The man and I both wore jeans and black T-shirts. We hugged a little awkwardly and sat down to talk over our drinks.

In the last nine months, though he was still struggling with writing, he'd applied to eight fully funded MFA writing programs across the country.

"That's great," I said, and I meant it, although I did think, with a chilly pang in my throat—that seeped down to my chest—*What if he moves away? It's my own fault for not getting together with him before.*

But I knew he needed this. More than he needed me, a woman he'd met on the Internet who hadn't called him for almost a year. He needed this the way I'd needed the last few months alone.

"Why did you call me again?" he wanted to know.

"David Bowie told me to."

"Oh."

"No, he really did."

The fact that he didn't get up and run right then told me something, for sure.

"Are you going to write about it?" he asked. "In that memoir I thought you should write."

"Maybe." I mentioned my David Bowie blog post, the first heartfelt thing I'd written in months.

"Sounds like he's your muse," he said.

I want to be yours, I thought but didn't say.

Two hours later he walked me to my car on the roof of the parking structure and said goodnight. As he turned away

I took hold of his thick canvas Dickie's jacket, the one that made his shoulders appear even broader, feeling the thick canvas bunch satisfyingly between my fingers, and pulled him back into my arms. And kissed him on the mouth.

"Can I see you again?" I asked. It felt like I'd just pulled off all my clothes and now stood there naked on the parking lot roof, my blemishes, scars, and wrinkles exposed by the lights of the city.

He paused, looking only into my eyes.

Finally he said, "Yes."

Maybe the Oracle's spell had worked after all.

If WRITING IS love, does that make writer's block the opposite? What if you'd never been loved properly as a child—how does that create an obstacle to your writing? What if your mother never hugged you? Brushed you away when you once tried to put your head on her shoulder as you fell asleep in the car clouded with cigarette smoke? What if you discovered that your father had another family in a different country, which explained your mother's tormented smile under her daisy-festooned Easter hat, but only in retrospect because as a child, how could you understand any of this?

What if your adult heart has been repeatedly harmed?

I believe I know the answer: Love and write anyway.

Love and writing originate from within.

They require sacrifice.

They are worth the wait.

Just like magic.

12 QUESTIONS FOR *THEIR EYES WERE WATCHING GOD* BY ZORA NEALE HURSTON

Janie Starks **wants** romantic love after being enraptured by the fecund beauty of a blossoming pear tree when she is sixteen.

She **needs** to find her identity without relying on a romantic relationship or on the way others define her. She needs to fully find her voice.

Her **gift** is her romantic nature, but taken to an extreme, her romanticism leads to her **flaw** of becoming overly dependent on the object of her affection. Likewise, her gift of idealism results in her flaw of naïveté.

Janie's **arc** takes her from innocence to wisdom and from dependence to independence and self-expression. Her true romantic nature becomes stronger as she develops her spiritual side.

Her **loving antagonists** are the men she initially relies on to fulfill her—the aptly named Logan Killian, Jody Stark, and her true love, the tragically flawed Tea Cake Woods. Her **big bad antagonists** are the racist and sexist people she encounters.

These same qualities of racism and sexism can be attributed to the Southern **setting**, which serves as another antagonist for Janie and pushes her along her arc.

The point of view moves from Janie to the antagonists to the peripheral characters, including, at one virtuosic moment, a flock of buzzards; this use of a third person POV serves as a **stylistic** device to enhance the **theme** of finding one's voice.

The use of dialect and colloquial language contrasted with Hurston's soaring spiritual prose illuminates the voice.

Janie's **crisis** is the hurricane that almost kills her and Tea Cake before he rescues her from the water and an attack by a rabid dog.

During the **climax**, Janie must shoot her husband when he attacks her. Another climax is reached at the trial, where she finds her voice, defends herself, and is set free.

The **resolution** brings Janie back to her home, remembering her beloved Tea Cake, and finding peace. ━━━━━━━━━━━━━━━━━━━━━━━━━━━━

THE 12 QUESTIONS: CLIMAX
Question #11: What is the climax of your book?

THE CLIMAX IS the most dramatic scene in your book. It almost always comes near the end of the story and pits the protagonist against the antagonist. Usually it has more action than any other scene and pushes the character to utilize his gift as the character reaches the culmination of his arc.

We change most, and perhaps most quickly, when we are forced to fight our fiercest battles. In the same way, our characters, who have been moving gradually toward change along their arcs, are able to fully transform after their own battle scenes. In tragic novels, the characters may not change, but the reader will understand the writer's message just the same.

Sometimes a climax is written in shorter, choppier, more verb-reliant sentences, with less interior thought or description, than the rest of the story. At this point in the book, the character needs to be taking action rather than ruminating.

HERE ARE SOME climactic moments from our sample novels:

> In *To Kill a Mockingbird*, Scout fights Ewell and is ultimately saved by Boo Radley, the false antagonist, as she realizes the true nature of good versus evil.
> In *The Great Gatsby*, the climax comes when George Wilson shoots Gatsby in the pool.
> In *Jane Eyre*, the climax takes place "off stage" when Rochester is blinded in the burning house.
> In *Play It As It Lays*, an incident that is alluded to at the beginning of the book—the overdose death of Maria's friend BZ—serves as the climax.
> In *Lolita*, Humbert's murder of Claire Quilty creates a climax.
> In *Wuthering Heights*, Heathcliff's death, brought on, ultimately, by his lingering grief over his loving antagonist, Catherine, brings the climax.
> (In these last two novels, both tragedies, the protagonists are not changed by the climactic events in the same way that the protagonists of other novels are, and yet the reader is still enlightened by the impact of the moment.)

In our own lives, we face not just one profound climax, but a never-ending series of them. I have found that by reading about the struggles of characters in novels, I feel less alone and more empowered to meet my own challenges. By writing about my own struggles through my characters' actions, I've also become stronger, and made connections with others who have faced similar adversity. **Try writing a climax that not only allows your protagonist to grow and survive, but also strengthens your own sense of self.**

10

THE THORN NECKLACE
—— Words into Action

F RIDA KAHLO'S *SELF-PORTRAIT WITH THORN NECKLACE*
and *Hummingbird* has become, for me, a symbol of the
pain in life and the healing power of making art. But, especially these days, we need more than just art to heal. We need
to take action in the world.

During my freshman year of college, trying to deal with
the depression and anxiety brought on by my father's illness, I trudged from my dorms, through the morning fog,
across the Berkeley campus to see a counselor in a rundown,
makeshift bungalow. The contrast of this environment to
the other stately palaces of education on campus made me
wonder how seriously the students' mental health was being considered.

With her early-Joni-Mitchell hair and eyes, the counselor resembled a younger version of my mother. I talked to her for a few weeks without revealing much before I finally broke down and began to cry.

"There's so much poverty and violence and pain in the world. I can't understand how we just go on with our lives when so many people are suffering."

She furrowed her brow and looked at me through the lenses of her glasses, kindly, but as if she hadn't fully seen me before.

"What is really going on with you?" she asked.

"My dad has cancer," I said.

I'd deflected my grief into overwhelm about the fragility of the planet. It was easier to focus on this than to face the idea of the loss of my father. But my sadness about the world was real, too.

> We need more than art to heal. We need to take action in the world.

No matter how much inner work we do on ourselves, there is still a globe of pain to contend with.

And it just keeps getting more complicated.

IN JANUARY 2017, shortly after Donald Trump was elected president, I attended the Women's March in Los Angeles. On that brisk, fresh-sky day, my friend Tracey and I met some friends downtown and tried to walk toward Pershing Square. But the crowds were so dense that we found ourselves in a standstill, backed up against skyscrapers, quite a few blocks away from the center of the march.

Even from this somewhat distant vantage point, though, we felt the positive and powerful energy envelop us.

If you tend toward claustrophobia, the best landlocked space to occupy is one full of pacifists. Not to mention radiant ones with pussy hats, pink hair, and ingenious signage featuring Maya Angelou's poetry, Nancy Sinatra's boots, Charlize Theron as Imperator Furiosa, and the Obama-nostalgia-inducing artwork of Shepard Fairey. I was especially touched by a woman with a T-shirt that read "Why I March" and an arrow pointing down to her pregnant belly, and a young boy standing on a wall above the gathering, looking out soulfully into his future.

In this case, a crowd is a comfort.

Here are souls who struggle as I do, one might think. *We worry about threats, the same threats, the same fears, the same injustices.*

In college, I'd attended my share of protests. After all, I'd chosen Berkeley, in part, because of its progressive history. Though I'd missed the heyday of activism and found most of the college culture revolved around the Greek system, I still had the chance to participate in an anti-Apartheid movement that called upon the University to divest from South Africa, and involved all-night campout protests on Sproul steps.

My loneliness was at its height on those nights of cold stone and distant stars, yet I felt I was at least attempting to make a difference.

THE 12 QUESTIONS FOR FRIDA KAHLO

Let's imagine we are writing a book about Frida Kahlo. How would a narrative story about Frida answer the 12 Questions?

The **main character** Frida's **childhood wounds** stem from contracting polio at an early age and then surviving a horrific bus accident as a young woman. In response to the pain and isolation of these experiences, she becomes a brilliant artist, able to transform her physical and emotional pain into passionate art.

Frida **wants** the love of her unfaithful but **loving antagonist** husband, Diego Rivera, as another way to ameliorate the pain, but when the relationship becomes too destructive, she **needs** her independence.

Mexico is the **setting**, offering a backdrop infused with the brutal imagery of its Aztec past. Its colors— shades of prickly-pear-magenta and electric blue— have a profound influence on Frida's art and **style**. Her elaborate, traditional, Tehuana clothing both hides her wounds and expresses her identification with her native country and its early inhabitants.

Many **crises** plague this character, including illness, surgeries, abortions, and Diego's many affairs, especially one with Frida's younger sister.

The **climax** pits Frida and Diego against each other. In that moment, just before her untimely death, he realizes the magnitude of his love for her.

The **arc** takes Frida from an obsessed, suffering woman to a fully realized artist forged and cauterized by pain. This journey imparts the **theme**, a message that temporal love can relieve physical and emotional pain for a time, but that the creative process can transform pain into something that will heal others for years to come. ━━━━━━━━

FRESHMAN YEAR, WHEN I returned home to visit my parents, the three of us went downtown to the inaugural demonstration for the Great Peace March of 1986. Protestors had planned to walk all the way from Los Angeles to Washington, DC. Once again my feeble father rallied and began to sway and dance to the band like a melancholy clown; this time his antics didn't embarrass me but only made me proud. I turned and saw a pair of palely blue and familiar eyes in the throng—it was my obsession, Smoke, six years before he would fall in love

> As humans, we all have our own necklace of thorns. But we also wear hummingbird charms among the brambles.

with me. I took this as another sign of our deep connection and it sustained me until that Ferris wheel ride where he finally recognized what I'd known all along.

The next day I flew back to Berkeley, embracing my father at the Burbank airport. "We'll do so many things together after you graduate," he said. He would remind me of this once more, in the letter he mailed the day he died.

But after that anti-nuke protest I never saw him again.

He passed away less than three months later, a few days after the nuclear accident at Chernobyl. I think this tragic event literally broke his heart, in much the same way that, perhaps, the great Leonard Cohen—romantic, brooding, highly creative, and of similar ancestry as my father—was in some part felled by the election of Donald Trump days before Cohen's passing.

What my father left me with was money in the bank, a letter telling me to live joyfully and without guilt, inspiration to a life of caretaking and activism, and the memory of his voice resounding in my head:

You are a writer!

It was only another expression of his love, and it inspired me to go forth and live a life in which I support and care for those around me with my actions and with my words.

WE MAY FEEL powerless and alone, with so many challenges before us. Which is why it's more important than ever to connect, speak up, share the truth, demonstrate, run for office, organize, donate, volunteer, break down hurtful boundaries, and let our individual voices be heard. And one of the best ways to do this is through creative expression.

Consider educating others by writing from your heart about issues of social justice and sharing your writing with like-minded souls. If you're not studying writing in school, you can still sign up for individual classes or critique groups or start one of your own. You can also try joining or starting a book group, as I still believe writers learn more from close reading than almost anything else. Try collecting your friends' writing and artwork and starting a zine or blog. You might even look into self-publishing. If you want to be part of a bigger support community, National Novel Writing Month (NaNoWriMo) is an annual online creative writing project in which participants write a minimum of fifty thousand words of a novel during the month of November.

If you've never had a father tell you that you are an artist; if it feels like no one believes in you or gives you permission; if you continually doubt yourself, but a voice inside still yearns for expression—you must listen. You must continue to create and not give up. Get support if you need it, and keep listening. That voice is telling you something, even if you don't want to hear: **You are an artist!**

Though creative expression has always been easier for me than life in general, writing continues to present its own challenges. When I am stuck in my writing, I run with my dog past the eucalyptus trees in the park and find jagged

> When I am stuck in my writing, I run with my dog past the eucalyptus trees in the park and find jagged fragments of bark scattered on the asphalt. They remind me of jigsaw puzzle pieces like the words of my book that need to be rearranged in my head and on the page to make a cohesive whole.

fragments of bark scattered on the asphalt. These remnants remind me of jigsaw puzzle pieces like the words of my book that need to be rearranged in my head and on the page to make a cohesive whole.

Moments of frustration, self-doubt, and despair plagued me as I wrote this book. Focusing on my body issues in particular has been almost as painful as the medical procedures I've had to go through time and again, especially as my eyes and skin and organs and hormones and joints and bones continue to face the ravages of age.

But through it all I remember that my vulnerable, self-exposing words may provide some solace for someone along the way, may encourage them to create as well.

As humans, we all have our own necklace of thorns. But we also wear hummingbird charms among the brambles—expressions of our yearning and our ability to transform pain into beauty and into love.

THE 12 QUESTIONS: RESOLUTION
Question #12: What is the resolution of your book?

BY THE END of your book, offer a resolution that shows your main character at the culmination of her arc and expresses your theme in the most effective way. If you're not sure how you want your book to end, consider your choices in a general way: Do you want a happy ending? A sad ending? An ambiguous one? Which best suits your story?

THIS IS HOW our classic authors resolved their stories:

Scout is safe and loved by her family, and she has a new friend—Boo Radley. Her heart is open, which will help her become an even more realized, mature adult as she continues to grow.

Gatsby is ruined by his obsessive loyalty to the memory of his relationship with Daisy.

Jane Eyre finds true love with Rochester, as well as a greater sense of self.

Catherine and Heathcliff are destroyed by the cruelty they have suffered.

Humbert and Dolores die, ruined by Humbert's perverse obsession.

Maria and Kate are reunited.

Note how all of these resolutions demonstrate the culmination of the characters' **arcs**, and are a direct expression of the writers' **themes**.

EVERYTHING IN THIS world eventually comes to an end. How can we give meaning to our short lives on this planet? **One way is to write stories that express our true selves to the world, stories that explore life's mysteries and connect us to others in a deep and compassionate way.**

SCENES

NOW THAT YOU have a very simple set of questions and answers to help structure your book, you can begin to write using the main building blocks of story: the scenes that populate the book. Scenes present a continuous action in one place and during one period of time with a beginning and end point.

The answers to the **12 Questions** provide the skeleton of your book; the scenes are the organs.

Let's think about scenes with the **12 Questions** in mind, as well as other elements of storytelling. A scene generally needs a sympathetic (**gift**) main character with a goal (**want**), an **antagonist** who often blocks or hinders that goal, and a central conflict created by the clash between these two characters that may lead to the main character changing or growing (**flaw/need**), even in a very small way, by the end of the scene (**arc**).

Every scene has its own **crisis**, **climax**, and **resolution**. You don't necessarily need an overt cliffhanger at the end of every scene, but you do want to end the moment on some point of tension. This will keep the reader engaged and motivated to continue reading.

Scenes take place in a defined **setting**, often the more conflict-laden the better.

Scenes employ many elements of **style**, including imagery and description, although it is important to introduce these selectively to increase tension rather than dilute it. A description of a flower's color and shape and beauty is *pleasing* to read, for example, but it will be more *impactful* if you describe it in terms of its temporal nature, the death inherent in all life.

Dialogue in a scene immediately grounds the reader in the moment. The spoken language should be natural and used to stimulate **conflict** and **develop character**, rather than just as an exchange of information or mundane daily pleasantries. Janet Fitch, author of *White Oleander*, feels that dialogue should almost always be reserved *only* for conflict. Dialogue can also build character, but the best way to do this is to show someone in conflict: That's when we see who they really are. Fitch also says that in each conversation, one character "wins." Who will win in your scene? Will your main character be closer or further away from getting what he wants?

A well-written scene **avoids telling too much with exposition**. Writing from the body is one way to avoid unwanted tells. How does emotion register in your character's head, eyes, throat, chest, pelvis?

Avoid clichés when describing these sensory responses. Warning: Sometimes writers can get so caught up in being original that they can't move forward. If you need to use a cliché as a placeholder, that's okay.

Although much of scene writing is "showing," we should also use "tells" in the form of **interiority** as characters express thoughts and ideas. Interior thought lets the reader understand the internal conflict as the point of view character experiences it. These philosophical "tells" are often the most quoted phrases from novels. They generally present the **theme**.

EXERCISES

1. Write your main character's **childhood wound scene**, the moment when your character was hurt in some deep way. This scene can appear at the beginning of your book, midway as a flashback, late in the story as a climax, or not at all. Whatever choice you make, this scene will inform your entire story.

2. Write an early scene in your book in which the main character **wants** something and pursues it. Set your character up against another character, one who does not want the main character to reach a goal. Rely on **dialogue** to demonstrate this external conflict and on interior thought to demonstrate the internal **conflict**.

3. Write a scene in which your main character ac-
    tively demonstrates a **gift** in a way that engages the
    reader. You can also hint at a **flaw**.

4. Write a scene in which your main character moves
    forward in their **arc** toward their **need**. You can
    write a scene where the character changes in a
    small way, which is usually how we change in real
    life. Or, you can write about a sudden, dramatic
    change; if you do this, you are probably writing the
    climax! Either way, use **actions** to demonstrate this
    external transformation, and **interior thought** to
    demonstrate an internal change.

5. Write a scene in which your main character encoun-
    ters a **loving antagonist** and changes just a little bit
    toward the culmination of her arc. Then, write a
    scene with a **false** or **big bad antagonist**. Notice how
    your character behaves differently when facing each
    adversary.

6. Write a scene where the **setting** creates a **conflict**.
    It might cause a problem for the character directly,
    or establish a contrast to the internal struggle of
    the main character. If you choose the first option,
    you will probably rely more on **action** to drive the
    scene, and if you choose the second option you
    may rely more on **interior thought**.

7. Print a few pages of your work and read them,
    starring what works and circling what might be
    improved. Then, analyze your **style**. What **adjec-
    tives** would you use to describe it? Is your style

classic, quirky, modern, upbeat, charming, lyrical, haunting? Do these adjectives reflect your main character and story? Are they the words you would want to appear on your book jacket when your publisher is describing your book? If they aren't, what can you change to make your style in sync with your story?

8. Choose a scene that you've written but you feel needs revision. Consider these techniques as you recraft the words:

> Is your **syntax** varied, not repetitive?
>
> Does your **diction** avoid repetitions and do you choose words that are consistent with the style of the book?
>
> Is your **imagery** and **figurative language** evocative and unique?
>
> Is the **point of view** most effective for the story you are telling?
>
> Is the **tense** consistent, or intentionally inconsistent? Would your book benefit from being in present tense instead of past tense, or vice versa?
>
> Does the **tone** of your writing reflect your main character's state of mind and the story problem?
>
> Is there a balance between **showing** and **telling**?
>
> Is your grammar reasonably intact? Are your pronouns related to their proper antecedents? Do the verbs agree? Do you avoid the passive voice? Are you using punctuation correctly?

9. Write a scene from the middle of the book, with your main character in **crisis**. Use **interior thought** to track what the character is feeling. How does this test the character and push him toward his **need**? How does it make him face his **flaws**?

10. Write a scene at the **climax** of the story. Show the **protagonist** reaching the culmination of her character **arc** through an encounter with an **antagonist**. How does this scene push the character to fully realize her **need**? How does it push the character to fully overcome her **flaw** using her developed **gift**? How does your **theme** present in this scene?

11. Brainstorm three possible **resolution** scenes for your book. One can be **happy**, one can be **tragic**, and one can be **ambiguous**.

12. Write a scene from your book that directly states the **theme**, either through **dialogue** or **narration**.

BONUS EXERCISES

1. Create a **fictional character** by answering the **12 Questions**.

2. Choose a real person and answer the **12 questions** for him or her.

3. Write (or rewrite) the first scene of your book:

    *   Use an initial **hook** that gives a sense of a central conflict, and perhaps the **antagonist**, and engages the reader right away. Both *To Kill a*

Mockingbird and *Play It As It Lays* use elements of the books' climaxes as the opening hooks.

- Identify a **setting**.
- Identify the main character's **want** and **gift**, and possibly his **flaw**.
- Make the character **active**, not just thinking about something. Poise the character at the beginning of her **arc**.
- Hone your **style** of writing because this will be what helps a reader decide if he wants to continue.
- Hint at the **theme** of your book.
- If your book has a **title**, insert a reference within the scene that clarifies the title's meaning.

AFTERWORD
—— The Magic Is Within

WHEN I FIRST BECAME A WRITER, I HADN'T YET DE-
veloped the **12 Questions**. But I had read a lot as a
child, and so I wrote intuitively, with myths and fairy tales in-
fluencing my structure and my characters. Eventually I came
to see how the 12 Questions applied to my own primary
character—and myself. After all, my character, Weetzie, is my
alter ego; what drives her comes from me:

Weetzie's **gift** is her ability to see magic and love in
the world. This is symbolized by the (literally) rose-
colored sunglasses she wears.

Weetzie's **flaw** is her inability to face reality and acknowledge the darkness in the world.

After experiencing the childhood wound of her father leaving, Weetzie **wants** love and a family of her own.

What Weetzie **needs** is to see her loved ones for who they really are. Her **arc** is from illusion to reality. She finds real magic when she faces the truth about life and balances light and dark.

Weetzie's big bad *and* false **antagonist** is the witch, Vixanne, who only sees darkness and helps Weetzie acknowledge the shadow. Her loving antagonists are her dad, Charlie, who forces her to see life's pain and temporality when he dies of a drug overdose, and her beloved boyfriend, Max, when he leaves her after she sleeps with her two gay best friends, Dirk and Duck.

The **setting** is Los Angeles, which embodies the beauty seen through pink sunglasses as well as the darkness of broken lenses.

Weetzie's lyrical, playful **style** is reflected in the voice of the narration but the choice of third person adds a little distance to make the story more mythic and universal rather than entirely personal.

The **crisis** or "dark night of the soul" is when Charlie dies.

The **climax** comes when Dirk finds Duck, who has run away.

The **resolution** is the reunion of Weetzie and her loved ones.

The **theme** can be expressed this way: If you face reality but maintain faith in the magic, you will be able to experience real love. Life isn't about happily ever after; it can be painful, but also, ultimately, happy.

All of these questions may be applied to the writer as well as the main character. Compare Weetzie's 12 Questions profile to mine:

My **gift** might be the ability to write through pain, no matter what, and to help others do the same.

My **flaw** might be to unconsciously push myself into pain as a way to find inspiration for my writing.

My **want**, based on a number of **childhood wounds**, has always been romantic love, to find love magick through a romantic relationship.

My **need** is to find the magic within myself.

My **arc** could be: from a lack of self-love to love, from not seeing the magic in myself to seeing the magic and being able to show others the way to find it within themselves through the creative process.

My **loving antagonists** are my parents.

Los Angeles is my **setting**, a character, a muse, and an extension of my voice as narrator.

My **style** is lyrical, fluid, moving back and forth through time, sometimes in intentionally disorienting ways.

My **theme**: The magic is within us. Use it to combat the pain.

My **crises** have been the painful relationships with a series of men, the deterioration of my health, and financial struggles.

One **climax** is my confrontation with the most negative of these men, symbolizing the self-destructive aspects of myself.

My **resolution**? Writing this book. For you.

ACKNOWLEDGMENTS

I HAVE NEVER written a book that has needed and received so much loving support. First, I'd like to thank my friends, colleagues, contributors, beta readers, mentors, and general sources of inspiration: Melanie Arriaga, Laura Lee Bahr, Lilly Barels, Jen Becherer, Molly Bendall, Lara Bennett, Scott Blackwood, Pablo Capra, Michael Cart, Diane Sherry Case, Stevie Cee, Jade Chang, Brandie Coonis, Joanna Cotler, Lisa Cron, Gala Darling, Tracy DeBrincat, Liz Dubelman, Samantha Dunn, Christine Ecklund, Brenna Ehrlich, Reina Escobar, Danishka Esterhazy, Janet Fitch, Sera Gamble, Amanda Yates Garcia, Maria Gillespie, Tod Goldberg, Adam Greenberg, Seth Greenland, Hans Hacker, Christine Hale, Denise Hamilton, Steve Heller, Sarah Herrington, Ashley Inguanta, Elgin James, Charles Jensen, Autumn Kimble, Allison Kramer,

Jim Krusoe, Stacy Lee, Edan Lepucki, Jessa Marie Mendez, Rhalee Hughes Perry, Robyn Peterson, Alison Powell, Alan Rifkin, Steven Reigns, Katy Rose, Nadya Rousseau, Chris Schuette, Amy Schiffman, Sasha Stern, Emily Sterren, Lauren Strasnick, Michelle Tea, Lorinda Toledo, Dr. Linda Venis, Alma Luz Villanueva, Diana Wagman, Daniel Weizmann, and Terry Wolverton. I learn so much from all of you. Dr. Carol Blake, Dr. Paul Crane, Dr. Adam Griffin, Dr. Pouya Dayani, Kanani Kroll, and Mia Togo, thank you for helping keep my body and mind strong and healthy enough to complete this task. Richard Nash, thank you for introducing me to my agent Erin Hosier, who pretty much single-handedly (with the legendary Betsy Lerner backing her up) made this happen! Laura Mazer, Amber Morris, Kerry Rubenstein, Matt Weston, Julia Campbell, Deb Heimann, and everyone at Seal Press and Hachette, I am deeply grateful that you gave me the opportunity to publish with you. Most of all, love and thanks to Mary Pauline Lowry, Laurel Ollstein, Tracey Porter, Gregg Marx, Gregory Tower, Jasmine, and Sam.

ABOUT THE AUTHOR

FRANCESCA LIA BLOCK is the Margaret A. Edwards Lifetime Achievement Award–winning author of more than thirty acclaimed and widely translated books of fiction, nonfiction, short stories, and poetry. She has also written a screenplay for Fox Searchlight and contributed essays, interviews, and reviews to many publications including the *New York Times*, the *Los Angeles Times*, the *Los Angeles Review of Books*, *Nylon*, and *Spin*. Francesca teaches at Antioch University in Los Angeles and UCLA Extension.